TREATMENT
CRIES THE BLUES II

THE SCIENCE OF ADDICTION
AND IMPULSIVE BEHAVIOR

LENDELL L JONES

O.C. ORIGINAL COUNSELOR

Copyright © 2023 Lendell L Jones. All rights reserved.

No part of this book may be reproduced, stored, or transmitted by any means—whether auditory, graphic, mechanical, or electronic—without written permission of both publisher and author, except in the case of brief excerpts used in critical articles and reviews. Unauthorized reproduction of any part of this work is illegal and is punishable by law.

ISBN: 979-8-88640-878-2 (sc)
ISBN: 979-8-88640-879-9 (hc)
ISBN: 979-8-88640-880-5 (e)

Because of the dynamic nature of the Internet, any web addresses or links contained in this book may have changed since publication and may no longer be valid. The views expressed in this work are solely those of the author and do not necessarily reflect the views of the publisher, and the publisher hereby disclaims any responsibility for them.

One Galleria Blvd., Suite 1900, Metairie, LA 70001
1-888-421-2397

Treatment Cries the Blues II details the progress of a group of diverse people who are going through therapy for a variety of problems. As the story develops, however, it becomes clear that the counselor is the one who needs counseling, as he faces problems with his ex-spouse, child support obligations, visitation rights, and financial difficulties. Throughout the course of treatment, the clients share their life experiences with one another and, in the end, help each other as much as they are helped by the counselors.

This challenging work deals with issues ranging from religion, suicide, incarceration, domestic violence, homosexuality, racial and economic discrimination, addiction, family separation, gangs, and friendship. *Treatment Cries the Blues II* will interest those looking to help a family member or friend as well as those who are interested in the dynamics of therapy.

CONTENTS

Dedication vii
Acknowledgment ix
The Personalities xi

Chapter 1:
18 and Life to Go

Treatment Cries the Blues II 3
This is a White World 5
I know! You Rich! Bipolar Person! 9
What's the Problem? 13
Antisocial Manipulation Plot 17
Gangster Love 20
Who's Angry? 24
Smoke-free in Maroon Village 28

Chapter 2:
18 and Life to Go

Gaining Courage to Set Boundaries 36
Hotline, Hotline, Calling on the Hotline 40
Too Many People Have Problems 42
Supporting Hurt Feelings 46
Don't Quit Before the Miracle Happens 50
Read my Lips: Spiritual Awakening 53
Smoke-free In Maroon Village 56

Chapter 3:
18 and Life to Go

I Can See Clearly Now the Rain is Gone 64
Clients' Discussion 66
Building Self-esteem 68

Building Self-Esteem 71
How to Build Self-Esteem 73
Precious Souls 76
It's Time to Get Honest..79
What is the Good Stuff? 82
Level I, II and III The Power of Change: A Discussion Activity 86
Smoke-free in Maroon Village..90

Chapter 4:
18 and Life to Go

He Doesn't Seem Right..100
Hope for a Better Day 103
Family Reunion 106
It's Called Bipolar..109
Future is Looking Bright..112
Is this the End?..115
Epilogue 119
Treatment Cries the Blues: A Cry for Help....................................123

Treatment Cries The Blues:
The Musical

Treatment Cries the Blues 128
Introduction..132
Act I: This is a White World 134
Act II: Gaining Courage To Set Boundaries...................................153
Act III: I Can See Clearly Now the Rain is Gone 171
Act IV: He Doesn't Seem Right...189

About the Author 215

DEDICATION

I dedicate my work to Shylisa and Brendon Jones. It is because of my love for you that I have committed to touch others' lives through the work of therapy.

I dedicate this book to my beautiful wife and helpmate, Kala. My commitment to you grows stronger each day. I thank God for blessing me with you each and every day.

"Ain't no woman like the one I got."

-The Four Tops

ACKNOWLEDGMENT

First and utmost, I thank God for the talent and the talented people in my life. My special love goes out to my two most beautiful children, Shylisa and Brendon Jones, and a special appreciation and thanks to my lovely and patient wife, Kala Jones. Without God and the support of my family, I would be lost.

In loving memory, I thank my late parents, Leonard and Mozell Jones, along with my oldest sister, Alice, and my youngest sister, Sonji La Fonda. My parents and sisters were always a source of strength in my life, and the wisdom they gave me is still helping to shape my life today. I also see and recognize my brother and my other sisters, who have supported and believed in me ever since I was a seven-year-old kid and wrote my first short story, "You Ain't Made of Glass." A special expression of my love goes out to my brother Raymond, and sisters Debbie, Sharon, and Lagail.

Make no mistake about it, I will forever acknowledge the people who keep Mission Impossible Counseling in effect.

The Impossible Crew:
- Larry Armstrong *(business manager)*
- Brittany Page *(editor and writing coach)*
- Daniel Arnold *(graphic designer)*
- Jeremiah Townsend *(marketing supervisor)*
- Neil Johnson *(pastor and stage plays director)*
- Chelsey Nelson *(CPA financial advisor)*
- Kylie Neagele *(research consultant)*
- Dr. Mary Katherine *(family therapist)*

Dr. Jim Armstrong *(clinical psychologist)*
Tonya Bockmon *(clinical supervisor)*
Sabrina Parson *(southern states, books distributor)*
Deborah Foutz *(clothing designs director)*

A BIG thank you to the Ute Mountain Ute Tribe and especially to the staff of Ute Counseling and Treatment. Y'all are wild! Yet I don't think I ever worked with a team who has more heart than the Ute Mountain Crew. Rock on!

A recognition shout-out to:

Four Winds Recovery Center, who gave me my start in 1992 – There will always be a special place in my heart for that agency.

Rebecca Jasper's and Associates – Thanks for showing me the inside scoop on how to diagnose properly.

A New Awakening – I appreciate your team for your continuous support for Mission Impossible Counseling, even when it seemed impossible.

To the crew of Family Crisis Center – Your team is solid. I enjoyed every moment working with you all.

Desert View Family Counseling Services – Thanks for working in populations up on the north side. Keep up the good work.

A moment of silence for the late Scott Davy of Davy and Associates. Scott was a true pioneer in the substance abuse and mental health field who taught me the outpatient scoop of counseling.

The Ewings Publishing Co. – Thanks for believing in my works and being the Hot Spot publicist.

Last but not least, thanks to the readers of my works. Your support is greatly appreciated. I write for you and try to touch on subjects of your interest. Only by the Grace of God and the readers is this made possible.

To everyone who has supported and believed in Mission Impossible Counseling, I thank you all from the center of my heart.

Oh yeah, I almost forgot. I'm sending out a super duper shout-out to Chelsey Nelson, Kylie Naegele, and Eugene and Bernice Cook. You folks are so groovy and a joy to be around.

God bless the world.

THE PERSONALITIES

Pazmate is a rich, egotistical person, who determines a person's place in life by how much money and material possessions they accumulate. Pazmate believes the other clients in treatment do not equal up to him, socially. He has a more in-depth dislike for Steve, who is an ex-caseworker. Pazmate is not shy about expressing his views and with every chance he gets, he tries to humiliate Steve with sarcasm and disrespectful remarks.

Julianne is a mother who has lost her children to the state's custody and continues to live her life in shame and self-blame. She presents herself as being flirtatious to escape from the pain and seek validation. Julianne has recently been diagnosed as bipolar and her character and emotions go from one extreme to another instantly.

Sharon is a white supremacist who holds tight to her beliefs that this country would be better off if all non-whites were banished. Sharon is put on a behavioral contract by her black counselor for calling a homosexual client, a faggot.

Mike Jones is a black counselor, recently divorced, going through child custody battle with his ex-spouse, and is having financial difficulties. His personal life frustrations have started to affect his performance at work. Mike has become distant and disassociated during his shift. Mike begins to wonder if he's really helping anyone and is contemplating suicide.

Ben is a homosexual whose father has refused to speak to him for over ten years. His father claims that Ben has embarrassed the family. Ben has recently found out that his father is dying of lung cancer.

Marty is a shy person with a borderline-avoidance personality. He seems to always be afraid. Marty's self-esteem is low and he has a hard time communicating with others. He has become painfully accustomed to cruel and inappropriate jokes towards him.

Steve is an ex-caseworker with a Mr. Know It All personality. Steve has become very good at understanding what is wrong with other people. However, he has a blind spot around how problematic his own life has become. Steve acts as if he and the counselors are peers.

Minnie is a gang member who represents the Dirty Crips 20s and has been affiliated since the age of twelve. Minnie feels that she must stay cold and tough in order to survive the game. Minnie likes to stay to herself because if faced with confrontation, she must prove her strength against them.

Charles is a thirty-nine-year-old ex-convict who has been in and out of jails and prisons for more than half of his life. Charles has anti-social personality disorder and finds pleasure in telling war stories. Charles has been known to charm and manipulate others, including professionals.

Terry is sixty-five years old and has been drinking heavily since the age of twelve. Terry has recently received her fifteenth DWI. Terry can't seem to understand why everyone is making a big deal about it; she's not a criminal. She pays her taxes. She deflects her crimes against the state, contesting that there are rapists, murderers, and robbers out there who are the real threat to society.

Pete is a forty-five-year-old who has a history of abusing his partners. He has been divorced twice and his most recent ex-girlfriend has a restraining order against him. Pete believes if women would just shut up and listen to him, he would have no need to abuse them. Pete believes the right man—him—can beat Minnie's disrespectful attitude out of her.

Skeety is a fun, attractive, female counselor who has deep concerns for the clients and staff.

Inky is a goofy male counselor who suspects something isn't quite right in the treatment atmosphere.

Tim, the treatment center administrator, shares information with the counselors.

CHAPTER 1

18 AND LIFE TO GO

People raised in functional or dysfunctional homes typically have a tendency to play out the family role and view the world through the eyes of the people most important and most influential in their lives. People raised within functional families generally learn from an early age how to govern their behaviors and are acceptable to constructive criticism as they can recognize inappropriate behaviors. People raised within dysfunctional families generally learn from an early age to blame others for their behaviors and are not acceptable to constructive criticism as they recognize inappropriate behaviors. Typically families have values; what's important here is, once becoming an adult, one has to discover which family value has or hasn't been working.

1. What family values I've learned as a child have worked against me?
2. What family values I've learned as a child have worked for me?
3. What behavior has worked against me and do I have the courage to change the behavior today?

TREATMENT CRIES THE BLUES II

A tall, slender woman with sandy blonde hair cascading down her back and green eyes shining behind thin, framed glasses, enters a dimly lit room. The clients' lounge of Mission Impossible Counseling Treatment Center.

"It's true. Somehow I had been slowly, secretly, and completely seduced by this treatment center. During my fifteen years of working here as a counselor, I have cried, laughed, cursed, and praised this treatment center. Yet, no matter the season, I can always count on my two closest friends, counselors Inky and Mike to help me celebrate or sob my pain away. Essentially, the three of us could be considered family. We have grown very close over the years; we even attend one another's family reunions and are welcomed as part of each other's families. At any rate, this is a treatment center and we are counselors. Like you, we realize how devastating addiction and maladaptive behaviors can be. We have discovered that people of all levels of society have the potential to be affected by addiction and maladaptive behaviors. Our jobs as counselors are to help position the clients we work with to identify the harmful situations, take ownership of their part in the situations, and then create a "change of lifestyle" plan that will benefit them and society. We are a sixty days program. We operate on a cycle of thirty days. This means we bring in and discharge twenty clients every thirty days. The program has a normal ratio of forty clients.

"Congratulations! We are starting a new cycle today. Why don't you read for yourself and get a feel of what sixty days of treatment is like at Mission Impossible Counseling? Hey, there's my buddy Mike! Mike, come here, I need to talk to you."

"Not now, Skeety. I'm running late. I have a new client waiting in my office."

"Okay running man, be gone. Oh yeah, Mike I almost forgot, I did see a young lady walking into your office about fifteen minutes ago. She seems so sweet. Inky told me her name is Sharon. You better not be too harsh on that sweet, little soul."

"I won't, I won't Skeety! Now stop talking to me. Like I said, I'm late—I'm late! I hope my new client won't have a bad impression of me because I'm late on our first appointment."

"Don't be silly, Mike. That sweet child is going to love you."

"Well, I don't know about loving me. I just hope we can get off on the right foot and have a healthy therapeutic relationship."

THIS IS A WHITE WORLD

A redhead stares at a colorful vase filled with wilted, purple iris on the desk and becomes agitated. Sharon has been waiting in his office, listening to the clock on the wall tick for what seems like an eternity. Plus, the more she looks at the bookshelf full of pictures of them—nappy-headed black kids and a big-bootied woman—the more she begins to dread what her primary counselor must look like. While she is still in dreadful thought, Mike, her counselor, enters his office and engages in an introduction with her.

"Hello, how are you doing?" Mike asks, extending his hand. She refuses it, tightening her grip on her folded arms. Mike takes his chair and tries again. "My name is Mike and I will be your primary counselor while you're in treatment. I trust you have been shown around the facility and have taken time to settle into your room by now," he says, though Sharon seems distracted by the prism of light her wristwatch has created on the floor. To avoid silence, he continues on.

"Sharon, if you haven't had the chance to meet all the other clients and staff, you will in due time. The staff here is very supportive and caring. If you have any questions about what is expected from you while in treatment, please do not hesitate. Feel free to ask me or any other staff member. This is my open invitation for you to discuss any concerns or needs you may have."

Mike opened a can of worms with that statement and gets a tinge of regret as her eyes finally meet his.

"I got a question," Sharon says. Before she can ask, Mike's mind begins to shift to treatment mode.

"Shoot," he says in a friendly, welcoming tone, hoping that the look on her face will soften if she understands that he is a friend, not an enemy.

"Do you really think I'm going to open up to you and tell you anything about my personal life?" she asks as though Mike's invitation were an insult. "Frankly, counselor sir, my life ain't none of your damn business. However, my brilliant, self-titled, probation officer came up with this genius of an idea that I need treatment. So here I am," she says as though it were a threat to him. "Howdy," Sharon says sarcastically.

Instead of using his normal approach and getting too therapeutic on her, Mike eases in on her, shifting down in his chair.

"You know, Sharon, it seems to me you're not happy to be here," he says, thinking that Sharon's eyes were going to get stuck in the back of his head as she penetrated them into his own and says, "Hey, yer quick! Didn't take you long to get it all figured out, did it?"

"No," he replies. "It didn't and now that we both agree that you are angry, what would you like to do about it? Yet, more importantly, how willing are you to work on addressing the core of your anger?"

"Counselor Mike, that's your name, right? You really would like to know why I'm angry and what makes me angry?" she asks, planting her feet firmly on the ground, her hands flat and sweating on his wooden desk.

"As a matter of fact, I would," he says, not backing down. "That is, if you don't mind being open and sharing with me."

"Niggers," she says coldly, as if the word rolling off her tongue had a bitter taste. "Niggers just like you." She states it slowly, to make sure Mike doesn't miss a single syllable and though he is surprised to hear it, he never gives Sharon the satisfaction of thinking it bothers him. Instead, he leans back in his chair and stares at her as though she were a painting with a tear in it. He stares out the window into the parking lot and watches Skeety walking to her car in the rhythmic way she always does as though she had a 1980s track on loop in her brain.

"So," Mike answers, returning to his job, "I understand that I make you angry, but what I do not understand is what behavior or action I am doing to trigger your anger."

Sharon rolls her eyes. She's heard these self-help, preachy lectures before. "I don't like you Mike and just by me being in the same room with you is making me sick. Is that so hard for you to understand?"

"Well, the good news is: you don't have to like me nor do I have to like you. However, one thing is for sure, you are in treatment and while you are here we might as well put our heads together and figure out the best plan so you will not have to come back to treatment, to me, or anyone like me again."

"Again?" Sharon can't believe what she's hearing. "I don't wanna be here now!"

"But you are here," Mike answers, keeping his voice cool in hopes to calm her fire. "I would like to inform you that we do not have locked doors here. Anytime you feel you would like to leave treatment, that is your choice," he says, gesturing to the door. "I also would like to advise you, if you would like to stay in treatment and work on the issues that led to the behaviors that brought you here, that's a choice too."

"Yeah right! Some choice. I wasn't born yesterday, I hope you know. If I do walk out those 'so-called' unlocked doors, the genius you think you are, you'd more than likely call my probation officer and I'll be back in jail."

"Now that you are realizing the power of choice, what choices are you willing to make for yourself to improve your situation?" Mike asks.

Sharon doesn't reply, but extends her legs out and stares at the sleeves on her folded arms.

"While you're pondering on that," he continues, "here's your first assignment in treatment." Mike gets up, walks to the bookshelf, and retrieves a three-ring binder with Sharon's name taped on the binding. "I need you to complete this feeling journal and return it to me in two days. That is, of course, if you choose to stay in treatment," he says, waving the journal in front of her. She takes this action as him toying with her, so she snatches it out of his hands. "Do you have any more questions for me?" Mike asks.

"As a matter of fact, I do," Sharon says.

"What's on your mind?" he asks, returning to his chair.

"Could I change counselors? I'd prefer a white counselor."

"No," Mike replies firmly. She's not happy. Sharon is sure that it's completely possible, but Mike wants to torture her. She thinks he enjoys the fact that she hates him and enjoys that she, a white woman has to answer to a black man. "For the time being, Sharon, it seems like you are stuck with me," he says confirming her thoughts.

I KNOW! YOU RICH! BIPOLAR PERSON!

Julianne, a twenty-eight-year-old woman with short brown hair, black-rimmed glasses, and an affliction for high heels and tight jeans enters the clients' lounge en route to her women's group.

She overhears one of the men, the good-looking one, Pazmate, say, "Steve, I noticed you were giving Charles advice earlier during the meditation group, but—I couldn't help wondering if you're really such a great counselor. I mean, if you were so good at it, and you *seem* like a guy who has great advice, why are you here in treatment with all the rest of us?"

"Pazmate, why don't you just back up off of him!" Julianne jumps in, always ready to defend the underdog. "At least Steve *tries* to be supportive. *You,* on the other hand, have not shared one thing about yourself, other than you have lots of money and you've come from a very wealthy family," she finishes taking a seat in the room, proudly crossing her legs and bouncing her dangling foot.

"And?" Pazmate asks sarcastically. "What is it you would like for me to share with you, Julianne? Would you all like it if I told you I was a poor, little, underachiever with parents who could not afford to pay their bills or that a loved one abused me?" He says while sarcastically rubbing his eyes with his fists. "Would I fit into your little world then?" He finishes sitting in a chair, pulling a GQ magazine out of his back pocket and opening it.

"No, Pazmate. That's not what we want to hear from you," Julianne says, taking the time to readjust her chair so that she faces Pazmate. "Really, we'd like to hear very little from you. However, I don't think it would hurt if you decided to cut the crap and accept the fact that even though you may have a lot of money, your substance abuse has caused problems for you and others. So apparently you couldn't buy your way out of that."

Pazmate doesn't want to listen. Instead, he pulls out his phone and surfs the Internet, pretending to be disinterested.

Steve, the insecure, somewhat stumpy, though well-built man jumps in shyly, "I have seen people like you fail at treatment time and time again." Pazmate isn't interested in what Steve is saying. Steve waits pensively, but once again, he's being ignored. "So would you like to know *why*?" Steve asks, daring to put his hand over Pazmate's cell phone.

"Not really," Pazmate replies jerking his hand away from Steve's.

"Well, today is your lucky day. I'm going to tell you anyway. It goes like this, Paz," Steve continues, rising from his chair and pacing the room as though he were addressing an entire audience. "There are certain groups of people who believe that they can control their outcome when they are under the influence of mind-altering substances and can not understand why other people make such a big deal about their using. What is happening Pazmate, and I suggest you pay close attention: That way of thinking blocks the avenue which allows valuable information to enter their brain, which is needed to comprehend a simple formula, allowing them to live one day at a time clean and sober."

"So tell me counselor junior, how long does it take a counselor like you to comprehend the simple formula?" Pazmate says, not giving Steve the satisfaction from looking up from his cell phone.

"Give it a rest," Julianne says stepping in between the two of them in an attempt to shake off their verbal attack on one another.

"Yes, Mommy Dearest," Pazmate says condescendingly, looking up from his phone just long enough to give her an amused look. "As much as I hate to miss the rest of you two's insightful conversation, I think I'll stick to reading my new subscription to Money Week," he says tapping his phone, "and bore myself with the details of how people of higher class don't understand the poignancy and sustenance of life as you lower class people allude yourself to believing." Pazmate gets up and walks out of the clients' lounge with a smirk on his face.

"Julianne," Steve says, empathetically. "I really feel bad for Paz. He just doesn't seem to get the simple formula that will no doubt make his life better."

Though Julianne doesn't care for Pazmate and his obvious disinterest in her, regardless of her efforts, she's sick of Steve's illusion that he doesn't belong there with the rest of them.

"You know," she says. "Pazmate is a jerk, but he is right about a few things."

"Oh yeah?" Steve replies, surprised. What could Paz possibly be right about?"

Steve likes Julianne. He thinks she's a little rough around the edges and her extra complex, emotional baggage is the type of women he usually avoids, but with the right man, a solid, responsible man like himself, he is sure she would soften up.

"Well for one, you do seem to come on as if you had the answers for everyone else, though I rarely hear you speak about your own issues or how problematic your usage has been." Julianne waits to see how Steve will take the criticism, but he only stares at the floor, rubbing the tip of his shoe into a paint spot on the tile. "Pazmate is right. You are very supportive toward the rest of us by identifying and addressing our problems, and we're grateful, but what about yours? This isn't my attack on you," Julianne says sitting in front of Steve. "I realize you were a caseworker for many years and helped many people to better their lives. That's really great. Still, I have to wonder, have to hear it from you—this formula, this idea that you are always talking about—does it ever apply to you and your own growth toward recovery?"

"Well, hey," Steve says fumbling, "I mean, that is a really good question and I would love to answer it for you at this time and give you some more insight on ways you can improve on all your day-to-day situations. Unfortunately," he says like an avoidant politician looking at his wrist for the time. "However, I still have my autobiography to write and I'm here to tell you that my primary counselor is strict. She's been riding me hard to get it done. So I guess I need to go and get started on it." Steve stands from his chair, fumbling to pull his jacket from its back and drapes it over his arm. "I'll be talking with you later on. Gotta run. I'll see ya."

WHAT'S THE PROBLEM?

Process group has always been hard for Terry. She finds it appeasing if she can be invisible and unnoticed during this time. Her many DWIs embarrass her. She's not some dumb kid anymore. She's sixty-five, lives in a trailer, and drinks too much. She lives a lifestyle only a college kid can get away with. She listens, like a shadow as the group talks to each other and makes herself as small as possible, hoping she won't be singled out.

"Hey, what about you? It's your turn to process your progression chart," Pete says, enacting Terry's worst nightmare. "You've been here a little over two weeks and still seem to have resentment toward the judge that referred you to treatment."

"I don't know what you mean," she says to Pete who is always trying to coerce her. She doesn't know why he hates her or feels like he needs to pick on her.

"Come on, Terry," Mike says trying to push her. "I think you know very well what Pete is talking about."

Men, Terry thinks to herself, sick of men singling her out.

"Okay, you want me to say it? Fine. Yes, I resent being here. How would you feel if you were treated like a common criminal?" Terry's eyes start to water, but she shields them by staring at the floor.

The group gets quiet. They'd never heard this woman utter two words and now she was on attack mode. They all look at each other and then at Mike who is the only one responsible to make sure she talks.

Mike shifts his chair so he can better face her and says, "Terry, would you like to elaborate with me and the rest of your peers as to exactly what you mean by 'common criminal'?"

She shakes her head slowly. Today is her day. She's sick of being labeled a drunk. Sick of the "loser" tag that people put on her and she's sick of being told what she can and cannot do. She's sick of people telling her how to live her life. She knows she's not doing anything glamorous. It's not as though when she was a little girl, she said, "I want to be a single, late-aged woman living in a trailer park with a dog who barely sticks around."

"Look, Mike, I admit I like to have a drink every now and then. But I am not an alcoholic nor do I have a drinking problem, so I don't see how it's a problem for everyone else."

Marty cautiously gives his peer feedback by saying, "Terry, I've heard you say on many occasions that you don't have a drinking problem. I've also heard you share about the fifteen DWIs you've received. Drinking and driving is very dangerous, plus it's an antisocial behavior—"

"Well, Marty, that's my point exactly," Terry fights. "Just because I choose to enjoy my life by having a couple of margaritas while driving, our so-called law enforcers feel like they have the right to promote a badge which reads, 'to protect and serve' the citizens of this great nation and apparently have nothing better to do than to harass law-abiding people like me."

"Yo, Terry," Minnie interrupts, sick of hearing Terry complain. "Instead of complaining and blaming the system for your mess-ups, maybe you should start taking some responsibility. If you don't want the cops bustin' you for DWI, don't do it. They'll leave you alone."

Terry isn't giving up the fight. She looks around at the group of people who are being spoon-fed about how they should feel and how they should behave and it makes her sick. No one is going to tell her she's wrong. It should be a personal choice. Isn't that what America is supposed to be about? She sits up in her chair, like a cat, on its haunches looking for a fight.

"I am taking responsibility," she yells. "It is my choice and my *right* to drink. I'm not hurting anyone or anything but myself and the last time I checked, that was still my right. Instead of wasting taxpayer dollars hauling me off to jail because I took a drive, our police committee should spend more time and taxpayer's resources apprehending people who are *truly* a threat—like gangbangers and common thugs." Terry falls comfortably back in her chair, feeling accomplished in her attack on Minnie. She didn't belong in a room with a person who is a violent criminal. Having a margarita while driving and mugging an old person for their purse and pimping hoes, in her mind, were leagues apart.

Mike, trying to get a hold of his group jumps in and confronts Terry, "Need I remind you that we are here to support one another's recovery, not to attack our peers when they give us feedback we don't like or agree with."

Before Terry can open her mouth and say another word, Ben speaks out by saying, "Besides Terry, you might not realize this, but you are fortunate to even be in treatment."

Terry gives Ben a condescending look. She refuses to conform to the mentality of the group and because of that, she feels like she is constantly being attacked. She won't let them fool her or take advantage of her just because she's in treatment.

"Yippy! Fortunate me," she says with little enthusiasm.

Ben looks her directly in the eyes and continues to try to get through to her. "You see my friend, the unfortunate ones never make it to treatment. They are the ones who end up in the cemetery, prison, or in wheelchairs. Let me tell you a true story about a real good friend of mine. He chanced it by drinking and driving and as a result, he killed a woman and her child who were on their way home from a Fourth of July barbeque. He is now serving twenty-four years in the state penitentiary."

The group grows silent. It always comes back to this argument. The argument no one wants to hear. The drunk driver who actually does kill somebody; the guy who only had a few beers and has to live his life with the guilt weighing him down and all the time in the world to think about it; the guy they think they'll never become. The group silently knows that each and every one of them has put themselves in a position that could kill another human being. They all secretly wonder what would happen if they had done it. What were the odds, really?

Would their families still support and love them knowing that their own irresponsibility, their accidental ignorance to the gamble of drunk driving had killed somebody? Is a drunk driver who makes it home safely any better than the one who hits and takes the life of another human being? Really, it all boils down to luck, right?

"Terry," Mike interjects. "We are out of time for this group. But I want to say that it took courage to process your progression chart with the whole group. I think you did well and hope you were able to take some of the feedback your peers gave you. Do you have anything else that you would like to get off your shoulder before we close this group?"

Terry shakes her head.

"Is there anyone who has anything more they would like to share with Terry?"

The group stare at one another while shaking their heads.

Mike wants to leave the group on a positive note. "I do want you all to be clear on the importance of giving feedback. What feedback is, it's a message you send to your peers that says—I'm hearing what you are saying and what you are saying is important enough to me that I will share my thoughts and feelings with you honestly in a loving caring way."

When no one interjects, he stands and says, "Okay, if there's no other feedback for Terry, let's close group in the usual way."

The group forms a circle, holds hands, and says together, "Hope for a better way, hope I will laugh and play, hope I will find the way, hope for a better day."

ANTISOCIAL MANIPULATION PLOT

Machismo, though taboo, is Charles' forte and career. He's a fraud who lives his life around a constant con and uses the people he comes in contact with as chess pieces in his elaborate plots. While Marty is doing his usual chores in the dining room, Charles decides he's going to use him as one more pawn to manipulate.

"Hey Marty, help me out," Charles says, entering the room and holding his stomach. Marty stands erect, sizing up the situation. "Man I don't know what it is," Charles continues, "but something I must have eaten during lunch really has my stomach upset." Charles sits on the couch like he was pregnant. "Normally it's not my style to ask favors from anyone, you know that, but today, man, I'll tell ya, I could really use a hand."

"What'd you need?" Marty asks, hesitant. He already has a day of rolling silverware and washing tablecloths ahead of him.

"How about sweeping and mopping the dining area for me?" Charles says, putting his feet up on the couch and turning on the T.V. "I just don't think I got it in me."

"Charles," Marty replies, rubbing the back of his neck, "I don't want you to be mad, however, my counselor and I have been working on me becoming more assertive and setting boundaries for myself," he says rolling another set of flatware. "One method we agreed on for me to start setting boundaries is to stop letting other people talk me into doing their chores." He keeps his head down, though he can feel Charles staring at him with a lowered brow.

"Come on, bro," Charles tries again. "I know you're not falling for that. Don't allow these counselors to run your life." Charles stands up and approaches Marty. He can feel Marty's insecurity seeping from his overlarge pores. "If you do, they'll brainwash you and run every aspect of your life. Is that what you want? You have to stay strong, little man. If there is one thing I'd learned while in the joint, hopefully you'll also learn this someday, it's us against them."

Marty thinks to himself, even if Charles is right he must stay as firm as possible. He never takes his eyes off the art form of folding forks into paper napkins. "Charles, I'm sorry. Maybe I don't understand the prison mentality and hopefully I'll never have to learn it." Marty finally picks up on his own flow. He takes his head away from his task and looks Charles in the eye, no matter how hard it is. "One thing I do understand is that I'm tired of the way I've been living, so if it takes brainwashing for me to live a happy, joyous life, well Charles, I hope these counselors brainwash the hell out of me."

Charles isn't done. "Little man, you are so weak. I've seen guys like you fall many times in the joint. You wouldn't last a week where I been."

"You know, Charles," Marty says grounding his feet onto the rug, "if you ever stop being your own enemy, you wouldn't have to go back to those kinds of places."

"Whatever," Charles replies. "You just don't get it," he says walking towards the utility supplies closet where the brooms and mops are kept. "Are you really that blind? You honestly can't see that all this is a conspiracy?"

Marty laughs, which only incites Charles' rant.

"Listen here, little man: the government wants us here in treatment so it can keep a close eye on us."

"Okay," Marty says, still laughing under his breath. "It's your story. Tell it as you want. Anyhow," Marty says, looking for an exit from the conversation, "I still have my relapse prevention packet that I need to complete by my next individual session with my primary counselor."

Charles crosses his arms across his chest, looking to continue the confrontation, but Marty finishes rolling the last of the silverware and wants to head for the exit. "I have to get going. I really do hope you start feeling better. I'll catch you later," he says heading for the door.

"You really think you have this thing all figured out don't you, little man?" Charles says approaching Marty. "But you'll soon see they're out to get you as well as me." Marty stands firm in front of him, but Charles is adamant on asserting himself. "You're blocking my way and as you can see I need to finish sweeping and mopping the floor."

"Saying 'excuse me' would be nice, don't you think?" Marty replies.

"Little man, there's no excuse for you. You seem to have been born that way."

"Throwing rude comments at me isn't going to help your situation. Why don't you try asking me to move in a polite manner?" Marty fidgets, but is fixed on not allowing Charles to push him around.

"Excuse me, little man, would you *please* remove your body from the path that I'm so desperately trying to clean up so I can get on with my day?"

"Of course, Charles," Marty says proudly. "I apologize for blocking your path." Marty steps aside, allowing Charles to finish his chores.

GANGSTER LOVE

Alone in the clients' lounge, Minnie is desperately trying to calm Ben down and support him while he processes the bad news he recently received about his father.

"I don't want to talk about it anymore!" Ben says, blocking Minnie's voice with his hands over his ears. "What part of that are you finding difficult to understand?" Ben sits down in a chair, hands still over his ears, giving a blank stare at the coffee table.

"Ben," Minnie replies, sitting on the coffee table, gently pulling his hands down. "I just want to know why you feel like it's your fault your father has lung cancer."

Minnie can see through his glazed look that he is suffering, but she can't understand why.

"Look," Ben says after taking a deep breath, "we've been friends from the first day we entered treatment together. I really do respect your 'little miss gangster booty,'" he says, breaking a smile, shaking a finger in her face. "But please, lose something honey, by keeping your pretty little nose out of my business when it comes to my family affairs."

Minnie's eyebrows raise. She can't believe she's being sassed when she's trying to help. "What? No, you didn't come at me with attitude," she says knocking his hand away. "I mean, I hear you," she says standing up and pacing to keep her cool, "and I'll back off, but remember I ain't had nothin' but love for you."

"Thanks, Minnie. You are such a *dear* friend and guess what—I ain't got nothing but love for you too, but this is my struggle, not yours."

Minnie wants to hit him. That's what she'd normally do, but when she sees him, bleached blonde hair buried between his fingers, she can't do it. "So where will you live when you leave treatment?" Minnie asks, taking the seat next to him and pulling his hand from his head, holding it.

"To be honest with you, I'm clueless."

"I would invite you to come and kick it with me . . ."

"Where? West Farmington! In the hood?" Ben asks, surprised.

"Like I was saying, 'Money' I *would*, but I *kind* of like you and *kind* of would like to see you stay alive."

"Minnie, you jive pigeon! Could you imagine me riding with the Dirty Crips 20s?"

"Honestly, Ben, I can't. Though maybe with a few alterations . . ." she says, trying to untuck his shirt.

"What? You think I can't fight?" he asks, trying to pull off her bandana. "Girl, I can sock someone in their nose and make it bleed and kick someone in their stomach and . . ." Ben says, standing up to take his victory dance with her bandana waving it in the air as though it were a scalp.

"See Ben, that's the problem," Minnie says irritated. She rips the bandana out of his hand as though he had tarnished something of sentimental value. She stares down at her bandana, rubbing her thumb across the stitchwork. "That is what most people think. Everyone thinks that all we do in the hood is go out and beat people up, rob, pimp, hoe, hustle, sell, and do drugs."

"Well—yeah," Ben says, waving his hand in front of Minnie's face. "Unless I've misunderstood something, you are a gang member, are you not? So if you are—"

Minnie jerks from his approach, taking an aggressive stance.

Ben tries to cool her down. "Minnie, put your fists back in your pockets. You're not exactly helping your case." He knows she's completely capable of using every ounce of her frame to beat the hell out of him. "Please correct me if I'm wrong, but isn't that what gangsters do—terrorize? You're the pirates of the twenty-first century. You fight and pillage . . . is that wrong for me to assume?"

"No!" she snaps, hesitates, "Well, yes. I mean, I don't know, sorta. Do you think I joined the Dirty Crips 20s because I want to hurt people?" she asks, afraid of the answer.

"I don't know," he answers. "I guess I never really thought about it. Why did you become a gang member?"

His question surprises her. Outside of her initiation, no one had ever asked her that before. She had to think about it. The reasons she joined seemed blurry to her now. How it started is not where she was now and it seemed to have snowballed on her without her really knowing when or how. Her eyes begin to tear up when she realizes she did it because she had to. It wasn't really a choice. At least, not in her mind.

"I became a gang member for the same reason people join the U.S. Army: to help defend and protect my neighborhood and the people who live in it. My family."

"Wow," Ben says, shaking his head. "Minnie, you know that's bull, right? You cannot convince me that illegal criminal activity in your neighborhood is considered patriotic."

"Look, man," Minnie says, getting passionate. Ben took it too far. "My mother . . . my poor, beautiful, sweet mother struggled to work two and three dead-end jobs at a time just to keep her family. My mother never brought harm to anyone her entire adult life! She was just walking home," Minnie says, looking for Ben's compassion. "We were always cold and hungry, so she went out to get us some marshmallows. We were going to pretend like we were camping."

Minnie's voice is hushed. Although she is standing in the clients' lounge at a treatment center, it is obvious to Ben that she is somewhere else entirely. Her eyes appear clear as a snow globe. She is shaken and through her dark eyes, he can see her story: a woman lying in the street, a bag of marshmallows fallen loose from a brown grocery sack, and three children staring out of the window of a dilapidated, one-bedroom apartment, snow falling, wondering where their mother was.

"I joined the Dirty Crips 20s when I was twelve years old. My aunt couldn't afford to take care of us all. I was the oldest, so . . ." Minnie snaps back to her place in time and wipes her eyes. "Anyway, I wasn't gonna let them get away with that. I wanted to make sure no one went through what my brother and sister did." Minnie stares at the floor, arms folded, and won't look at Ben.

Ben nods. He approaches her and places his hands on her caged frame. "Your family experienced hard times and a tragedy. You turned to organized crime, which I think I understand why, but that doesn't make you a patriot."

"That's your opinion," she says proudly. "But I'm here, protecting my own, just like the U.S. Army."

"Would your mother look at it like that?"

"Screw you," Minnie says, her globes filling with hate.

"Okay," Ben says, releasing his grip on her. "It's your story. Tell it how you like."

She won't reply, Won't look at him.

"Okay," Ben sighs and exits the room.

WHO'S ANGRY?

Nothing seems to frustrate Pete more than a loudmouth female that is clueless about Genesis and what the serpent did in the Garden of Eden. Minnie is hitting his last nerve.

"Yo, are y'all feelin' me because that's the way it is, dogg," Minnie says, finishing her complete autobiography with the group. She likes the attention of the group and finds her "hood rat" exterior gains her the attention of her peers.

"Who you calling a dog? Do you see any dogs in here?" Pete says, mocking her. "Speak English."

"You better back off me," she says aggressively. "I'm not in the mood for this, you heard?" In all honesty, Minnie isn't used to people standing up to her. Where she comes from, a voice, even a small one, can be punished if she is disrespected.

"Did I hear that you haven't said anything other than garbage? Yeah, I heard."

Minnie is up in arms, but Pete makes sure to rest calmly in his chair to prove that nothing about her or her demeanor upsets him.

"Both of you need to calm down," Mike warns.

"Hey," Pete says to Mike. "I am getting tired of this gangbanger running off at the mouth every time we come into groups."

Mike tries to comment, but Minnie interrupts.

"So what're you gonna do about me and my mouth, Pete?" Minnie challenges.

Pete laughs, treats Minnie like a joke. "You may have all these women around here scared of you," he says pointing to every woman in the group plus Ben, "but let me clear something up for you: I'm not one of them."

Minnie's eyes grow cold and black. She wished they weren't in group, but in a back alleyway in her neighborhood. Pete can see that he is infuriating her and continues to poke at her.

"It's women like you who make men like me abuse women," he says adding a smile. "What you need to learn is how to keep your big mouth shut," Pete says, clenching his fists. He knows he can't hit her, not here, but that's what she needs so he'll hit her with his language.

"Wrong!" she says, getting out of her chair and into his face. The embrace was immediately intercepted by Mike, who feels like a sheet of paper trying to block the river of a broken dam. "You abuse women because you are too afraid to confront a man. You beat women because you are a gutless coward."

Pete's face turns cherry red and looks as though he's going to punch Minnie in the face. It's her words now that have punched him. He jumps up out of his chair and screams, "You little bitch!" he starts, ready to teach Minnie a lesson. Steve jumps up from his chair and puts a firm grip on Pete to help Mike tear the two apart.

"That's enough," Mike warns again, but this time makes it more personal by adding, "I do not want to hear another word from you, Pete, and that goes for you also, Minnie."

The two contenders look around the room as though they had both forgotten that they had an audience. They both go back to their corners and the group is momentarily silent, waiting for something or someone to change the subject.

"Pete kinda has a point though." Minnie can't believe what she is hearing. "Don't get me wrong, I don't think it's okay to raise a hand to a woman, but—some of us get really tired of Minnie's way of communicating. Some of us don't understand all that homeboy and homegirl way of talking," Sharon adds, more than willing to express how she feels about the recent conversation between Minnie and Pete. Minnie gives Sharon the evilest look she can muster which makes

Sharon nervous. Attempting to diffuse the animosity, Julianne stands up for Minnie.

"I don't think a man should be abusive to a woman under any circumstance."

"I couldn't agree with you more, Julianne," Mike adds, grateful to hear a change of topic. "The fact is though—no human being should abuse another under any circumstance."

"That is so true. In my field, when *I* was a caseworker I saw abuse from both genders and the main ingredient that leads to abuse is uncontrollable anger," Steve adds, always happy to chip in his expertise.

"You know, Steve, you are absolutely right," Mike says. "The first step toward stopping abusive behavior is to start with the way we think. Once rational thinking is attained, people usually stop behaving out of their emotions."

"Wait a minute," Sharon chides back in. "It sounds like you're saying that true emotions are bad."

"No, I'm not saying that at all," Mike replies. "Let me clarify my meaning." Mike isn't even sure what he means anymore. How can he sit in a room full of people and tell them how to feel, how to rationalize their thoughts when he sits at his desk day in, day out, trying to rationalize his own? He rubs his temples with both hands, thinking it will help him understand his own life. "Sometimes," Mike continues, "our emotions can confuse our thought patterns which can lead to poor choices. And that can be confusing. It doesn't always work," he smiles. "Sometimes you spend so much time rationalizing your emotions that you forget what is real and what's not. Sometimes . . . sometimes . . ." Mike looks up and realizes that his group members are all staring at him, their eyebrows raised in wonder. "Okay," he says looking at his watch. "This group has run over schedule. Does anyone have any questions or comments before we close?"

"I do," Pete says, raising his hand.

"Yes, Pete?"

"I think I understand. I feel I can't always distinguish between reality and my own interpretation of reality. It isn't easy."

"I'm glad this was helpful for you," Mike answers with a slight sense of accomplishment. "Any more questions or comments before group close?" When no one chips in to the conversation, Mike starts the closing for the group. "Okay, then let's close with 'Hope for a Better Day.'"

After the closings, Mike asks Pete and Minnie to stay behind. "After this group, I need for you to go and talk with your primary counselors about your behaviors in group today."

Minnie and Pete look at each other; however, this time it is not in disgust, but more of an acceptance of their behavior like two children in a playground who shamefully know they've misbehaved.

SMOKE-FREE IN MAROON VILLAGE

(Two friends walk through their village in Farmington, New Mexico discussing and gathering information about smoking habits. While on their journey, they are intercepted by Grandpa Leonard.)

Brendon
Hey, Grandpa Leonard. I see you're still walking every day. Keepin' in shape?

Grandpa Leonard
That's right, young people. A strong body contributes to a strong mind.

Shylisa
Well, I believe in exercising, but my teacher says that going to school keeps my mind strong.

Grandpa Leonard
That is the typical way of thinking for the new generation of people and true. However, so many of us have forgotten or flat-out ignored the traditional Maroon Tribe way of life.

Brendon
That way of living might have worked for people back then, but these are new times.

Shylisa
I mean really, Grandpa Leonard—I don't mean to
be disrespectful, but things have changed.

Grandpa Leonard
I agree with you on that. Things have changed, but people have not.

Brendon
What do you mean?

Grandpa Leonard
Hear what I'm saying, little ones. From the time man has
been on this planet, he needed survival reparations.

Shylisa
Wait . . . I'm getting lost in what you are trying to tell us.

Grandpa Leonard
Be patient, child, and listen to me as I explain it to you.
Survival reparations are what we all need to live. And this
consists of water, food, air, love, and the Great Spirit.

Brendon
What does this have to do with what's going on today?

Grandpa Leonard
It means that if we don't remember how to use the
earth's resources wisely, we will continue to live
a crazy lifestyle that destroys our planet.

Shylisa
Grandpa Leonard, you are wise. I think I'm
beginning to understand what you mean.

Grandpa Leonard
Good, because it is true that a healthy body
helps us make healthy strong decisions.

Brendon
Well, it was nice talking with you, but we have to
go, Grandpa Leonard. Catch you later.

*(The two friends are considering Grandpa Leonard's wisdom
as they wave goodbye to him and go in different directions.)*

Shylisa
Dude, you are not going to believe this!

Brendon
Believe what?

Shylisa
My mom almost caught me smoking last night.

Brendon
What? Stop playing. How? You must be slippin'!

Shylisa
Whatever, I don't think so. It's like this though—I
thought my mom would be at my Aunt Alice's playing gin
rummy 'til at least ten o'clock. So Jerrica and me are up
in my room chillin' with the Marlboro Man, right?

Brendon
Right.

Shylisa
Then all of a sudden, just like that, I heard my mom entering through the front door.

Brendon
Dang! I bet you must have coughed up smoke. I mean, what'd she say? Did your mom smell smoke or something?

Shylisa
I don't know if she smelled anything, but if she did, she didn't say anything to me about it.

Brendon
Yeah, buddy! You must be feelin' pretty lucky about right now, huh? I mean you came *that* close to being busted.

Shylisa
Actually, I don't feel lucky at all. You know, the reason my mom moved us back to the Maroon Village from Albuquerque was to get us away from all the air pollution. It's kind of ironic that my mom moved me away from the smog when I'm smoking.

Brendon
What you talkin' about, Willis?

Shylisa
I'm talking about this smoking stuff. It's not worth hurting my family or me. I just don't know if smoking is the right thing to do.

Brendon
I feel ya, but do you worry about what our group of friends will say if you quit? They'll call you a buster.

Shylisa
I know that, but is smoking really right for me? Is it worth it?

Brendon
Yeah. You might be right, but where can we go to find the answer?

Shylisa
We can go and ask the Cigarettes. I'm sure they can tell us what a smoker or someone around second-hand smoke can look forward to.

Brendon
Okay. Let's go. Come on. I think I see the Winston Man. Surely he can give us some useful information.

(While the two friends travel on their journey towards the Winston Man, they are intercepted by the Drunkard Woman and her friend.)

Drunkard Woman
Hey, youngsters, come here. Come and have a drink with me. I have this magic potion here to drink that will make you go crazy and take away all your pain, fear, and absolutely all of your loneliness.

Shylisa
No thanks. We're in search of finding information about the dangers of smoking.

Drunkard Woman's Friend
Come here! Alcohol can be your best friend for life. Don't leave us. We don't like to drink alone. We need more friends.

Brendon
Well, have you tried a twelve-step program to help you quit drinking and find positive friends? Shylisa and I don't have a problem with alcohol, but Shylisa was almost caught smoking cigarettes last night by her mother.

Drunkard Woman
Come on! Come on! Smoking goes well with alcohol. See what it has done for us?

(The Drunkard Woman shows off her dirty clothes and stained teeth. The Drunkard Woman's friend does a little drunk dance.)

Brendon
Hey, I really feel bad for you two and I hope you will accept help some day and walk down the Red Road of Sobriety. But right now, we need to go talk with the Winston Man. Bye, my people.

(The two friends give the Drunkard Woman and her friend a brochure on the danger of alcohol and continue their journey. Moments later, the two friends walk up to the Winston Man.)

CHAPTER 2

18 AND LIFE TO GO

People raised in functional or dysfunctional homes typically have a tendency to play out the family role and view the world through the eyes of the people most important and most influential in their lives. People raised within functional families generally learn from an early age how to govern their behaviors and are acceptable to constructive criticism as they can recognize inappropriate behaviors. People raised within dysfunctional families generally learn from an early age to blame others for their behaviors and are not acceptable to constructive criticism as they recognize inappropriate behaviors. Typically families have values; what's important here is, once becoming an adult, one has to discover which family value has or hasn't been working.

1. How well did my parents communicate and support one another emotionally?
2. How well did my parents communicate and support me emotionally?
3. How well did my family as a whole communicate and support each other emotionally?

GAINING COURAGE TO SET BOUNDARIES

Having a defensive reaction in treatment is common and Julianne is having an especially hard time accepting her primary counselor's feedback. Julianne meets with Minnie in the clients' lounge to discuss her issue with her counselor.

"I can't believe she wants me to stop spending time with my male peers," Julianne says, banging the cabinets, looking for coffee filters. "This is treatment? I thought this is where we came to *practice* our social skills," she says to Minnie, who is cleaning underneath her nails with a pocket knife. "The way I've learned, being social means having the ability to communicate with people. It doesn't matter if they're male or female."

"Julianne," Minnie says, putting her blade back into her sock, "did your primary counselor request you to stop socializing with males completely? Or did she ask you not to socialize with them exclusively?"

Slamming the cupboard, she says, "What the hell is that supposed to mean? It's not as though I'm sleeping with any of them. These guys really aren't my type."

"I really hate to shake you off your throne," Minnie says, getting to her feet and pulling the coffee filters from underneath the sink where Julianne has been unable to find them. "But the way I see it, your type or not, you do seem to spend most of your time hanging on the men."

"Does that bother you and the other women? Am I detecting a little jealousy from you, sweetheart?" Julianne says, pushing her "assets" in Minnie's face.

"Bother me?" Minnie sputters, knocking Julianne's breasts out of her face. "Yeah, right. Why should it? Where I'm from—we keep it real," Minnie boasts, representing her colors, in place of her female attributes. "I'm just trying to kick a little flavor to you."

"Look," Julianne says, realizing her boundaries, "I know you don't mean any harm. I know you're not trying to attack me, but the truth is—I feel more comfortable around males than females. I just seem to trust men more. Women are scandalous and to be honest with you, I don't trust very many of them." Julianne pours her cup of coffee as though she resents it, dumping sugar and powdered cream into her cup and violently stirs it with an innocent, red straw.

Minnie takes a seat next to Julianne after filling her own coffee cup and tries to re-approach her friend.

"I think you're confusing trust with manipulation. You don't need to worry about me being scandalous. I ain't got nothin' but love for you. Girl, I'm not going to con or pamper you. I'll stay real with you. I'm not one to fall for the, *I trust men more*, trick. You shouldn't either."

"What do you mean?"

"Come on, Julianne," Minnie says, reclaiming her previous seat, "when you stick your 'assets' in men's faces and speak in that sweet, helpless, naive voice, you have men tripping over their own feet to serve you. I see you do it all the time. You can get what you want from men in ways that don't work with women."

"That's not true!" Julianne says, standing in defense. "See, now you're trying to clown on me."

"Hey," Minnie says, pointing out Julianne's contradiction. "Wasn't it you who said you don't trust women because they're scandalous? I'm trying to be straight with you. Your denial is making it very hard for me to trust *you*."

Julianne thinks about what Minnie has just said. She's busted and she knows it and instead of hiding her truth, she allows herself to be vulnerable to another woman.

"You're my friend. I would never try to intentionally con you, but my primary counselor has no right to insinuate that I'm male-dependent. It makes me mad when she thinks she knows what's going on in my life better than I do. Do you understand? I don't want to be that person she's making me out to be."

"Julianne," Minnie says, taking her friend's hand and coaxing her to sit. "You don't have to be anything you don't want to. Has it occurred to you that your primary counselor cares more about you than you're able to? She's looking out for the well-being of your children and wants to stabilize your abilities which will help you get them out of foster care. Maybe she's actually trying to help you get your children back."

Julianne's eyes are set on her hand tucked neatly between Minnie's fingers, but her heart is somewhere else. "I love my children. I realize I've made terrible mistakes as a mother. I'm ashamed of what I've allowed myself to put them through. I just don't know if they will ever forgive me—if I even deserve it. And if they do, I don't think I can ever forgive myself."

"You can," Minnie says, squeezing Julianne's hand. "All it takes is working on one behavior at a time, one day at a time."

Charles walks past the open doorway and upon seeing Julianne, enters, hoping to get her alone.

"Hey, Julianne, how about helping me with my relapse prevention packet? I've been putting it off long enough."

Julianne looks to Minnie who gives her a supportive smile. "Charles," Julianne says. "I think your primary counselor is more qualified to help you."

"That's cool. How about walking a few laps around the track with me to get a little exercise?"

"No," Julianne says with a pleased grin. "From now on I think I will walk with the girls."

"Game of checkers later?" Charles persists.

"Goodbye, Charles," Julianne says, waving a coy hand.

"Damn, what's gotten into you?"

"Goodbye," she says firmly, as if saying goodbye to a bad habit. Charles gives Julianne a nasty look to let her know she isn't worth the effort and exits the room.

When Minnie is sure their conversation will not be heard, she says, "My girl! That's the way. I mean, it was a little harsh, but you're getting there." Minnie jumps off the couch, giving Julianne a high five and hugs her. "And by you setting your boundaries straight, it will strengthen the relationship between you and your kids, bringing you one step closer to them."

"Thanks for being a friend," Julianne says, taking a serious tone. "Thank you for saying all of the things I needed to hear, which I feared, and for trusting that I had the courage to embrace them."

HOTLINE, HOTLINE, CALLING ON THE HOTLINE

It's a thin line between serenity and turmoil. Let the reader pause for a minute and pray not only for ourselves, family, friends, and neighbors, but let's also pray for the salvation of the world.

"Hey, Mike, perfect timing," Skeety says, seeing Mike in the hallway. "I wasn't sure if you were still here."

"Yeah, still here," Mike answers. "Another day in paradise."

"Line one is for you. It's your ex-wife," she says forcing a gritted smile. "I was just making sure you were in the building."

"Thanks," Mike says, sarcastically. "Transfer it. I'll take it in my office."

Mike sits at his desk, looking at the red, pulsing light on his phone. He rubs his face down to his chin before picking up the line.

"Hey . . . This really isn't the time to talk about this. . . . What do you want from me? . . . You know I can't afford to pay more child support. . . . What does that have to do with anything? . . . Why would you even want to keep our children's dad out of their lives? Why can't you get on with your life and leave me alone? . . . And ya' know, another thing—when you need to talk with me would you please call me at home? I don't bother you at work. . . . Why? Why? Why do you continue to blame me for your unhappiness? *You* were the one who walked out of the marriage. . . . Do you have any idea what you are putting the children through? Our children are scared to death of *that* man and *you* have them living with . . . yes him! . . . This is not about you. It's not about me. This is about me trying to protect our children from a possible lifetime of unresolved hurt. . . . What? . . . What is that supposed to mean? . . . Are you serious? . . . You're sincerely trying to convince yourself that I'm upset because you are with him? . . . On the contrary. I am *happy* the two of you are together. However, I'm very afraid when I think about the dangers you're setting our children up for. . . . I wouldn't have dreamt in a million years that someday I would be in a battle with my ex-wife, fighting to keep our children out of harm's way. . . . You know what? Do what you feel you need to do, but remember, our children are the ones who will ultimately pay the price! . . . Whatever . . . Bye! And please stop calling me at work—"

Mike slams down the phone and leans back in his chair, covering his face with his hands, taking deep breaths. After collecting himself, he sits forward, takes the picture frame with his children within it, and stares at the image.

TOO MANY PEOPLE HAVE PROBLEMS

Sharon still doesn't understand why the judge sent her to treatment which is predominately occupied with black people. Yet, as much as she dreads being in this environment, here she is, walking into Counselor Mike's office again for an individual counseling session.

"Sharon, come in and grab a seat," Mike says, offering her a chair. As always, she sits, slouched in her chair, with her legs extended, feet folded over each other. "Would you like to tell me what's going on?" he finally asks.

"Tell you what?" She asks nastily. "Sorry, but I don't know what you're talkin' about."

"Sharon," he begins again. "We are not going to play this little game today." Mike is tired and though he knows he must persevere, he doesn't feel prepared to help Sharon. "You know exactly what I'm talking about."

"Are you referring to my conversation with Ben?"

"Bingo," Mike replies. "And now that we are both on the same page, you can tell me why you felt the need to attack Ben." Though mostly hidden by her hair, Mike can see her eyes welling behind her thick, red locks. Before answering, she quickly wipes her eyes.

"I didn't attack Ben," she says, defensively. "I called him a faggot. He's gay. That makes him a faggot, doesn't it?" She smiles to let her counselor know she is in fact, pleased with herself. Mike, for the first time, can see a hint of Sharon's pain; the hatred her life has stemmed from and the caged bird whose song has been muffled out.

"Sharon, that kind of language is not acceptable," Mike says, pulling a form from his desk drawer. "And to ensure that you will not use such language like this again, I am putting you on a behavioral contact."

"What?" Sharon snaps, but Mike stays firm. "This place is really screwed up. You counselors tell us to be honest and give honest feedback and when we do, we are put on a behavioral contract?"

Again, the tears are coming and he can see into every tear that runs down her cheek that she hates him, but more importantly, she hates herself.

"First off," Mike stares at her before taking a deep breath. "Let's not talk about 'we' behaviors," he says, making quotation marks with his fingers in the air. "Let's stay focused on *your* behaviors. Tell me, by calling Ben a derogatory name, how is feedback such as that supporting him?"

"He's gay," she professes, throwing her arms into the air. "You're a God-fearing man. Are you telling me that you don't have a problem with that?"

"Sharon," Mike says, irritated with her word choice tries to calm himself. "We are not here to discuss what I have a problem with, but we can discuss how Ben being a gay male affects your recovery."

Sharon shakes her head. She is trapped in a world where no one understands her and worse yet, will not let her be. She's tired of making excuses for herself; she's exhausted having to answer questions on every, tiny, minuscule thing she does. "It's neither just nor right! It's disgustin'. It's Adam and Eve, not Adam and Steve."

"So what I think I understand is that you disagree with the way that some people live their lives," Mike says, playing Devil's Advocate. "That's fair. However, once again, how does the lifestyle of others affect your recovery?"

Sharon doesn't really have an answer, but won't let her black counselor feel like he has won a session, so she continues with what always works—sarcasm: "Well, I guess if the whole world became like Ben, it would cure the world's population problem."

O.C. ORIGINAL COUNSELOR   TREATMENT CRIES THE BLUES II | 43

"Sharon," Mike says, emotionally exhausted. He stands from his desk and begins to pace his office. "I have heard you speak of having a problem with different races. I have heard you speak of having a problem with one of your peer's sexuality, and I've even heard you speak of having a problem with the judicial system."

"Your point?" she interrupts as he stares out the window.

"My *observation*," he replies, "is that I have not heard you speak much about Sharon and her problems. Your probation officer did not recommend you to treatment because everything is wonderful in your life. Does that sound right?"

"There really isn't much to tell about me, Mike," Sharon says, staring at her shoelaces.

"You know, Sharon. You are right where you suppose to be."

Sharon looks up at Mike, giving him a look of hatred. "Oh really? How did you come to that conclusion, Mr. Counselor?"

"Let me simplify it for you, Sharon," Mike says, placing his hands on the desk. "Most people do not come into treatment doing cartwheels and back flips, demonstrating how happy they are here to be here. But you are here and it's up to you how you are going to use your time."

Biting her lower lip, she asks,

"Does my probation officer have to know I was put on a behavioral contract?"

"Yes, madam. The probation office will be notified by the end of the day. I also send out weekly progress reports." Mike can see that Sharon's chin is puckered and he actually feels bad for her. "Just remember," he says, trying to comfort her, "a behavioral contract is your agreement to discontinue the negative behaviors that led to it in the first place, not a statement condemning your progress."

"My probation officer is such a jerk," she says, allowing a tear to fall. "He always sends people back to jail. I'm just gonna end up . . ." but she can't finish her sentence.

Mike nods his head. "I notice you discovered another person with a problem, Sharon." He knows his statement is going to anger her, but he has to push her.

"They're not too hard to find, counselor," she says, sneering at him. Mike feels lost. Maybe he can't help her. Maybe she's not for him to help. Either way, he's tired.

"Anyhow," he says, wanting to end the session. "If you sign this behavioral contract right here, we'll bring this session to a close."

"Good," she snaps, leaning over the desk and sloppily signing her name. "I'm tired. These individual sessions are pointless!"

SUPPORTING HURT FEELINGS

Pete and Terry are in the dining room finishing up their dinner while engaging in a pleasant conversation. When the two become comfortable with each other, they are able to embrace their insecurities about their behaviors and about treatment.

Terry wanting to have a moment of clarity with another person starts a conversation with Pete by saying, "I really have been thinking about what my peers and counselors have been saying to me. I'm beginning to see that just because I haven't physically hurt anyone or myself, it doesn't excuse my reckless behavior while drinking and driving." Terry pokes at an olive on her plate with a fork, hoping she won't be rejected. Pete has never been her favorite person, but she raises her eyes to meet his. Pete chides in. "This treatment stuff is kind of hazy to me, but I believe this place is helping me understand my emotions better. I know it probably sounds funny but I didn't know I had emotions. I am so glad my primary counselor helped me understand the importance of making amends to Minnie. She and I get along so much better now."

"I don't mean to overstep my bounds," Terry replies, "I realize that I am not your primary counselor, so stop me if you'd like but . . ." Terry stops to take a breath, afraid that her question will offend her new friend. ". . . could you tell me how you felt when you became abusive towards your partners?"

Pete puts his fork and knife on his plate and says, "Shame. A lot of shame. I really don't mind you asking me because I've recently learned that I usually mask my shame with anger."

"So, have you discovered what triggers the shame?" Terry asks. She herself was in an abusive relationship many years ago and feels that that relationship is why she shut herself away from men, relationships, and the world. She wants to know why men hit; she wants to know why her husband hit her.

"Well, my counselor and I have been working on that. I think my insecurities stem from feeling like I'm not good enough. I was always comparing myself to others, while at the same time, trying to be a perfectionist. It made me lash out. When I was having feelings of inadequacy, I felt that she could feel it too; like she knew it and I hated that. It's almost like—" Pete stops, stirs the remaining noodle on his plate with the fork and tries again. "It was like she became my flaw. I projected it onto her and by hitting her, I think—I was hitting myself," he said it almost as if it were a question.

"What would happen when you were not able to live up to the high expectations you placed on yourself?" Terry asks.

"To be completely honest with you, I would explode and usually look for the weakest target."

"Your wife?"

"Anyone, really. Anyone who cared about me: parents, children, spouses, close friends. You name it, they were all fair game."

Terry fidgets with her napkin, trying to understand why Pete would pick on those who loved him, though she is really remembering coming home from work and her husband's anger. It could be anything: she'd cook them a meal and he'd start in on her because he didn't like the way it tasted, smelled, or even the texture of the broccoli made him violent. "It doesn't make sense, why would you rage on people who care for you?"

Pete can't understand why Terry's eyes are tearing up, but he continues on.

"You're right, Terry. It doesn't make sense. My insecurities made me feel safe, I guess. I figured if they really cared about me, they wouldn't hurt me or reject me, no matter what I did. So much for that old way of thinking, I'm now beginning to understand how hurt people have the potential to hurt others and the cycle I was living in."

"And it became a vicious cycle. Shame turns to anger and so on," Terry adds, fighting back tears.

"Yeah. That's how a cycle tends to work. Uncontrolled anger has the tendency to affect many lives; it has no borders or boundaries. Anger at its peak is like a tank at war, ya know?" Pete says, playing with a breadcrumb on the table. "Its mission is to destroy all that stands in its way. I guess the good news is I've discovered that anger is usually a secondary emotion. So much of the time, people use anger to protect their primary emotion or feeling. It's like, it's in our nature to defend ourselves even when we're our own attackers. We defend rather than listen and understand. I have learned from my counselor that the primary emotion or feeling could be hurt, fear, a feeling of being unloved or sad. I think what I've been doing is instead of expressing the core primary emotion or feeling, it's more comfortable to express my secondary emotion or feeling which in my case, is anger. I guess the main reason why secondary emotions are prevalent amongst many people is because their insecurities will not allow them to identify their strengths and weaknesses. By identifying these attributes in myself, it will help me to better handle stressful situations. Now that I understand more about myself, I have begun working on my insecurities by identifying my strengths and weaknesses. I can honestly say I seem to be making positive changes in my life. And ya know what? It feels really good."

"That's great," Terry replies with a wet face and a smile. Her friend's newfound confidence makes her own struggles seem more possible. Though she can never forget what her ex has done to her, she now feels like she can begin to understand him and if she can do that, then she can forgive herself. It wasn't her all those years. It was him. "I'm happy you are able to identify your attributes, Pete. I see them too. You know, I hated the judge who sent me to treatment, but now that I'm here, this is the best thing that happened to me since . . . I don't know when."

For the first time, in over a decade, Terry begins to feel a sense of community that she was sure was lost to her forever.

"Tell me about it," Pete chides in. "I have learned so much about me and my anger since being in treatment. I don't regret coming here. Of course, if you tell anyone I said that, I'll deny everything."

The two companions look at each other and smile as if they both know something the rest of the world has yet to learn.

DON'T QUIT BEFORE THE MIRACLE HAPPENS

Ben hasn't felt like this in years and the very thought that his father is actually coming to see him, has Ben in a frenzy.

"I am so scared," Ben says pacing the rec. room, settling into a chair across from Charles, standing up and quickly sitting back down. Charles smirks behind his newspaper and asks, "Scared about what?"

"Haven't you heard?" Ben asks excitedly.

Charles shakes his head and smiles, folding his paper and laying it on the end table.

"My *parents*. My parents are actually coming to see me tomorrow."

"Your mom and dad? No kiddin'."

"Yes. Yes, both of them!" Ben says standing back up looking for something to occupy his hands.

"So why are you scared? I thought you wanted your parents to come to family day visit," Charles says, dealing out a hand of cards, so Ben will sit down and quit pacing. Ben hesitates, but takes the cards and sits back down and stares at his cards.

"I do, Charles, I do, but—my father disowned me ten years ago when he found out I was gay. What are we playing here?"

"Texas Hold 'Em. So why do you think they are coming to see you now?" Charles asks, swapping the occasional card from the deck.

"I'm not sure. I found out through the grapevine two months ago that my father has been diagnosed with lung cancer." Charles' brow raises and he's ready to comment, but Marty walks in.

"Hey, what are you two talkin' about?" Marty asks, looking to get into the potential card game.

Charles takes the cards from Ben and begins dealing out a new hand. "Ben was just telling me his parents are coming to see him tomorrow."

"That's good news," Marty says to Ben, taking his seven cards. "What's the game?"

"Go fish," Charles replies, lying a card, face up on the table.

"I know," Ben says pulling a card from the stack. "I'm really excited but on the other hand, I don't know how I should feel."

"Well, have you tried with your hands?" Charles says, sarcastically. "That always seems to work for me."

"Oh, Charles, stop it. You know what I mean. I'm freakin' out here!"

"Are you still afraid that your father won't accept you for who you are?" Marty says, asking Charles for a five.

"Go fish."

"I guess that I am," Ben replies. "The last time my father spoke to me he said some hurtful things to me."

Charles, getting cocky about his hand says, "Ben, the one thing I have learned while in treatment is that I have little control over other people and what they think about me."

"Thanks," Ben says, knowing his hand is not a winner. "I know what you mean by that and you're right. I don't control other people's actions any more than they control mine, but it would mean the world to me if my father would just hug me and tell me he loves me."

"Yeah," Marty adds, trying to get a glimpse of his opponents' cards. "Well, who knows, come tomorrow your father may have had a change of heart. People do change—sometimes."

"Thanks," Ben replies. "Thanks for trying to cheer me up," he says to his friends.

"Well, you hang in there and stay strong, little buddy," Charles says slapping the back of Ben's shoulder.

"I will," Ben smiles.

"Remember," Marty adds, revealing that he is out of cards. "Don't quit before the miracle happens." Marty smiles, showing his cockiness at his talent for Go-Fish.

"Ah, son of a . . ." Charles says, throwing down the remainder of his cards.

"I won't." Ben stands up, not caring about his lost hand. "Thanks again for all the feedback and encouragement." His friends give him four encouraging *thumbs up*. "I think I'll go sit in my room for a while and try to envision what my day will be like tomorrow."

READ MY LIPS: SPIRITUAL AWAKENING

Can you believe it? Pazmate and Steve are alone in the clients' lounge and may put their childish behaviors aside and get serious about their treatment. God is good.

Steve paces back and forth, biting on his thumb nail, resenting the way Pazmate treats him. Pazmate's lack of acknowledgment drives Steve crazy and he finally has worked up the courage to confront Pazmate.

"Look," Steve finally says, bracing his hands on the back of a chair. "You seem to have an issue with me. I don't know where it stems from but I was hoping that you might have suggestions on a way we can resolve it." Steve lets out a sigh as though he's just gotten something major off of his chest, but as he should have expected, he doesn't get what he wants in return.

"What would make you think I would waste my valuable time having issues with someone like you?" Pazmate retorts, not taking time to look up from his cell phone.

"Sarcastic remarks like that, for starters," Steve says, not giving up.

Pazmate realizes that Steve's newfound confidence isn't going to go away, so rather than try to avoid it, Pazmate decides to turn it into a game. "Well, let me bring myself down to your class level," Pazmate says.

Steve takes the seat next to Pazmate and tries again. "I may not have as much money as you do or come from a financially wealthy family such as you, but when it comes to class . . ." Pazmate puts his phone in his shirt pocket to give Steve's insult its full attention.

Steve sees that he's pushed it too far and falls back a notch. "You know what? I'm not even going to go there with you today. I'm trying to call a truce with you."

"A truce?" Pazmate asks, apprehensively. "Are you kidding? You're the one who's been walking around here flaunting the fact that you're an ex-caseworker and who has an answer to what is wrong with the rest of us. I really don't think that's fair, sport. Do you?"

Now that Steve has Pazmate's attention, he's starting to regret it. Pazmate stares at him through his dark, brown eyes, and won't let go.

"Maybe you're right, Pazmate. Maybe I've been avoiding my personal issues by projecting onto my peers. I think it's my way of escaping from my problems, but—I am trying to be honest with myself and others by opening up to my counselor and peers."

"Good. You really are, 'junior counselor,'" Pazmate says, sarcastically. "You know, for a short moment there," he says rising from his seat to leave, "I was actually falling for your clever out-of-body spiritual awakening scheme. Real nice. You should get a job in the con industry."

As Pazmate is heading for the exit, Steve says, "I'm not trying to con you."

"What?" Pazmate asks, rudely.

"My recovery," Steve replies, shyly. "It's more important to me than that. I feel that if I start getting honest with others, well, maybe—we will be a stronger unit." Steve feels foolish opening up to Pazmate. He stares at the floor, waiting for Pazmate to destroy him. But instead, Pazmate lets out a big sigh and reclaims his seat across from Steve.

"Look," Pazmate says, digging through his vocabulary and trying to find a way to not sound too insulting. "Hey, look man, I'm glad you decided to, ya know, get real with yourself."

Steve is reluctant to share his feelings with Pazmate. He sees now that maybe he didn't choose his timing well to share with a new confidant, but he can't stop now. Boldly Steve says, "I can't believe I'm going to say this, but I really am learning something from this place."

Pazmate nods, reluctantly. He would hate to admit, out loud anyway, but he understands what Steve is saying.

"So—do we have a truce then, Paz?" Steve asks, extending his hand.

Taking a moment to think about it and looking around to see if anyone is witnessing this friendship, Pazmate extends his hand. "Truce."

Steve is ready to leave, but Pazmate decides to open up. "You wanna know something else?"

Steve nods.

"Being filthy rich, handsome, and *extremely* smart isn't all what it's cracked up to be." Pazmate finishes with a big grin.

"I guess I'll have to take your word for it, Paz," Steve replies, laughing. "I guess until I become filthy rich I'll just have to settle for two out of three."

Pazmate smiles. Steve walks over to the counter to place his old coffee cup into the sink and Pazmate realizes this may be his one opportunity to open up to another human being. He has to start somewhere.

"Hey," he says, getting Steve's attention. Steve turns and looks at Pazmate. "On the serious side . . . hey—I know at times I've been known to act like a jerk, but I really do think you're all right. I apologize for giving you a hard time."

"You know, Paz, you're not so bad yourself—once you get your head out of the clouds."

"Obviously," Pazmate replies. The men smile at each other, both knowing that they're a step further in their recovery. "Anyway," Paz says, looking at the time on his cell phone. "I need to go work on my relapse prevention project," he says, rolling his eyes. "I'll catch you later." Pazmate stands and exits the room. After he is far down the hallway, Steve says, "Yeah, catch you later."

SMOKE-FREE IN MAROON VILLAGE

Shylisa
Hey, Winston Man. How are you today?

Winston Man
I'm a little choked up. Other than that, I'm doing well. And you? What are you two troopers up to?

Shylisa
Brendon and I are out in the community gathering information about tobacco. Could you give us one good reason why a person should continue or start smoking?

Winston Man
Well, uh, let me think about it—I got it! Because—nope, that's not a good reason. How 'bout—no, that's not good either. Can we make this easier by letting me give you more than a few reasons why a person shouldn't smoke?

Brendon
Okay!

Winston Man
For your information, cigarette smoke is suspected to contain cancer-causing substances. Many of the nearly four thousand chemicals in cigarette smoke are harmful to people. Some are even suspected to cause cancer. Children that breathe

second-hand smoke are more likely to have: ear infections, wheezing, and coughing spells. Furthermore, bronchitis and pneumonia have also been suspected from smoking behaviors.

Shylisa

Thanks, Winston Man. But we're going to find another tar head that could tell us what's good about smoking.

Winston Man

The truth is, there's nothing healthy about smoking. People who smoke get sick more often. Plus, it takes them longer to get well, and that can lead to absentees from school and work.

Shylisa

Winston Man, Brendon and I are trying out for the basketball and track team this upcoming season. Can smoking interfere with our performance?

Winston Man

If the truth is to be known, athletes know that smoking keeps them from doing their best, by prohibiting them to perform at a level of their full capability.

Brendon

Well, thanks for the information. We'll think about what you've said. Bye now.

(The two friends continue on with their journey.)

Brendon

Hey, look! There's Ms. Kool. Let's go ask her.

(While the two friends continue on with their journey toward Ms. Kool, they are intercepted by Gangster Money and Gangster Cents.)

Gangster Money
Yo' what's up shorty? Where you shorties goin'?
How would you troops like to roll with some real
players and be down with a safe family?

Gangster Cents
True dat! Because we hold it down and protect ours.

Gangster Money
Think we don't?

Shylisa
No thanks! I feel safe enough with my own family.
Anyhow, we're going over to see Ms. Kool to get
information about the dangers of smoking.

Gangster Cents
Seems to me, you shorties are really thinking seriously about
your future. Good luck. I hope everything works out for you.

Shylisa
Thanks. I also hope you two realize that there is
more to life than gangbangin' and set trippin'.

Gangster Money
We've been contemplating.

Brendon
Good. And I hope your thoughts lead you two into action
which will get you out of the gang life before it's too late.

Gangster Cents
I feel you. Much love.

Shylisa
True dat. Much love to you back.

Gangster Money
Bye now. You shorties take care.

Brendon
Bye.

(The two friends give the gangsters a brochure on the dangers of gang life, and then leave the hard-core gangsters standing there. Moments later, the two friends are intercepted by Kylie relaxing on a blanket, reading a book in the community park.)

Shylisa
Hey, Kylie. What's up? What book are you reading now?

Kylie
Oh, you have got to read this book. It's called "Treatment Cries the Blues II." And not only is the material in this book well-written, the author whose name is Lendell L. Jones once worked here in Maroon Village as a substance abuse counselor.

Brendon
That's deep. Have you ever met the author?

Kylie
No. Although my mother has and she told me stories about how he would work out every day at the recreational center to keep his mind and heart strong. He always said to her that exercising regularly helped him be a better counselor to the people here in Maroon Village.

Brendon
So what is the book about?

Kylie
It's kind of deep! But if you really want to know, this book is about the science of addiction and impulsive behaviors.

Shylisa
Whatever, Kylie. Whatever that means. What happened to you? I remember the time when you wouldn't read a stop sign and now every time I see you, you're reading a book or something.

Kylie
Well, for the longest time I fooled myself and others by believing I'm just another person in the village that will never amount to anything.

Brendon
Oh my goodness, Kylie. I never knew you felt that way.

Kylie
Don't feel sorry for me! That's how I used to feel, but ever since I started seeing Mrs. Chelsey at social services, she has introduced me to a whole new way of thinking and believing that gives me a better view of myself.

Shylisa
Speaking of sorry, where's your dog Fluffy?

Kylie
She's with Mrs. Chelsey.

Shylisa
I felt so sorry for her when I found out she became lost in Shiprock for almost two weeks. I bet she was so afraid and hungry.

Brendon

I still remember the day you brought that dog home from the pound. Fluffy was the most pathetic-looking animal I have ever seen in my entire life.

Shylisa

Kylie, you have so much love for Fluffy. She is now one of the most beautiful dogs here in the village.

Brendon

So anyway, where is she?

Kylie

I asked Mrs. Chelsey to drop her off at the veterinarian this morning for her yearly check-up.

Shylisa

That's cool. You really love that dog.

Kylie

I do. I really do love Fluffy and did you ever know I saved her life? Fluffy was scheduled to be put down the day after I brought her home. And in a strange way, I feel somehow she also saved my life.

Brendon

I guess we will let you get back to your book and I think the changes you have made in yourself are wonderful. Keep up the good work.

Kylie

Thank you. I will.

(They give Kylie a high five and continue on their journey. Moments later, the two friends walk up to Ms. Kool.)

CHAPTER 3

18 AND LIFE TO GO

People raised in functional or dysfunctional homes typically have a tendency to play out the family role and view the world through the eyes of the people most important and most influential in their lives. People raised within functional families generally learn from an early age how to govern their behaviors and are acceptable to constructive criticism as they can recognize inappropriate behaviors. People raised within dysfunctional families generally learn from an early age to blame others for their behaviors and are not acceptable to constructive criticism as they recognize inappropriate behaviors. Typically families have values; what's important here is, once becoming an adult, one has to discover which family value has or hasn't been working.

1. As a child, was your family considered financially poor and needed outside financial assistance?
2. As a child, was your family considered self-sufficient and did not need outside financial assistance?
3. As an adult, would you consider yourself poor or self-sufficient with no need for outside financial assistance?

I CAN SEE CLEARLY NOW THE RAIN IS GONE

Skeety, Inky, and Counselor Mike are having fun and clowning on the clients and each other in the staff office.

"Hey," Skeety says, taking a seat next to Mike. "I hope you're ready to start your lecture on time," she says sarcastically while looking at her rhinestone watch.

Mike stares at her in wonder. She continues by saying, "I just walked past the group room and noticed all the clients heading that way. You know how much joy clients get by watching the staff in hopes they will catch one of us slipping up by showing up late for group."

"I feel you on that one," Mike says, folding up his newspaper and setting it on the table. "After all these years I still find it interesting how much time some of the clients spend observing the staff's every move, while they should be investing that same energy into their personal recovery."

"Excuse me," Inky says, laughing and placing the book which he had previously been buried in, down. "You both are talking as if our clients came into treatment with healthy lifestyles and boundaries."

"Yeah, I suppose you're right," Skeety says. "But come on, be honest, don't these clients get on your nerves even a little sometimes?"

"Most definitely, yet we are the professionals here, remember?"

Mike, wanting to take Inky off his high horse says, "Well, thanks for the class on professional ethics, Inky. However, the last time I checked, expressing feelings and thoughts in a comfortable confident way was considered to be healthy and bold." He smiles confidently, assured that he has set Inky in his place.

"Hmm, absolutely, that's right. That's why I'm confident in keeping my adorable colleagues grounded by reminding them in a healthy and *bold* way: who are the professionals and who are the clients," Inky says.

"However did we ever allow ourselves to be suckered into this conversation?" Skeety says, looking at Mike.

"Don't get me started," he says, looking at his watch. "I guess that's what happens when you're not busy working with clients and keeping things in order like you and me." Inky rolls his eyes. Mike takes it a step further to make sure Inky is silenced. "And judging from *example*, when you're not busy and keeping things in order, you'll have time to think of a lot flaws about the other counselors."

"Hey, thanks for pointing that out," Skeety replies, standing up and putting on her jacket. She sings, "I can see clearly now the rain is gone."

"Wow, who sings that song?" Inky asks. "I haven't heard that groove in a while."

"Johnny Nash. Nice, huh?

"Oh, yeah. You should let *him* sing it," Inky says, laughing.

"Haha. Yes we know you have jokes," Skeety says.

Mike begins laughing in with Inky, and sick of being picked on, Skeety decides to take her exit. "You two are having too much fun in here. Let me get out of here before I pass out from laughing. Haha," she says exiting as the other two are left behind—still laughing.

CLIENTS' DISCUSSION

The clients are preparing for a lecture in the clients' group room and have taken to clowning on the counselors and each other.

"Here we go again," Charles says to Sharon as he takes a seat in the semi-circle. "Another fun-filled, stupid lecture-filled day in treatment."

She half-smiles and nods, but Charles wants more out of the conversation. "So, what, you think all the lectures they give us are helpful?"

"Oh, no. I'm with you," she says. "Do these counselors really think they are helping us?" she scoffs.

"Hey, I don't mean to be third wheel in the conversation," Pazmate says, half-whispering to Charles and Sharon. "Honestly, I think most of these counselors are only here for a paycheck. I'm willing to bet a popsicle that some of these counselors drink and get high."

"Wow," says Ben, who has now caught on to the conversation. Taking a sip of coffee he adds, "That's a pretty serious accusation. Just a thought: have you ever thought that maybe they actually care enough that they will give their time and effort, providing we come with the proper attitude so that they can help us readjust our lifestyles?"

"You know, you could be right," Minnie says, dropping her feet onto the table. "Course, the other part of the story is that these counselors can't teach me anything that I haven't learned on my block."

"Yeah, right," Steve says under his breath.

"I'm sorry?" Minnie asks Steve. "Is there somethin' you wanted to say, Counselor Steve?"

Steve, not allowing her gang influence to intimidate him says, "That's a hell of an education, you've got from your block."

Minnie, wanting to pounce on him but realizing how little her gang status means here and how the others seem to support Steve, calms herself down.

"Whatever," Minnie replies, though she's thinking that maybe it is time to check out her other options. She always thought she'd be a badass. No matter where she went, she figured her colors would represent her. She began to question how long those colors were going to represent her rather than her, representing herself. She's not sure that's what she wants anymore.

Terry interjects and says, "Not in my wildest dreams would I have ever imagined I could be this happy being in a treatment center. I almost don't want to leave."

The group laughs together.

"I gotta say," Marty says to Terry, "I've never seen you glow as much as you have in the past week. You look so much happier than when you first arrived here."

"Thanks," Terry replies. "I'm real glad it's noticeable. I kinda got to the point where I figured as long as I was here, I might as well try to gain something out of it. How about you, Pete?"

Pete takes a minute to think about it, rubbing the bristle on his chin. "Well, it has done me good. I figured out that I don't want to spend my life in fear of being out of control of my emotions . . ."

"Shh," Minnie says. "I hear the counselor coming."

Julianne, who has been brooding since the beginning of the conversation finally opens up and lashes out at Charles who was disrespecting the counselors. "Personally," she snaps, "I enjoy gaining new information I receive from the lectures and I don't think they are stupid at all."

"Whoa, take it easy, cupcake," Charles says, defending himself. "What's gotten into you? You sure know how to bust a guy in the chops."

"I just think—"

"Shh," Minnie repeats herself. "Mike's coming."

BUILDING SELF-ESTEEM

Mike steps into the clients' group room wearing his Mission Impossible Counseling sweat suit, catching the attention of all of his clients. They're used to seeing him in stuffy business suits built by JC Penney, but now he looks clean, comfortable, like himself.

"Good evening, folks," Mike says enthusiastically. Hoping that someone will comment on his fresh clothes. "How's everyone doing on this nice sun-shining Thursday?"

"I'm doing well," Steve answers, thinking Mike looks like an idiot. "And you?"

"Thanks for asking," Mike answers, rubbing his hands together and taking his seat. "I'm doing well also."

Mike looks around the room and sees that he is not dealing with an especially enthusiastic group. They're slumped over with their arms crossed around their chests, watching their shoes pivot from side to side. "So," Mike says hoping to get the group motivated, "now that we have all the formal greetings out of the way, let's get down to business." He waits for a laugh but doesn't get it. "Today's topics will primarily focus on self-esteem."

"Self-esteem?" Marty says, feeling like he's at a Deepak Chopra convention.

"That's right," Mike replies. "Would anyone like to share with the group as to what self-esteem is?" Faces all staring at the floor, he addresses Pazmate. "You're looking smart today. Why don't you share with the group."

Pazmate feels like it is an easy question to answer and replies, "Self-esteem is how a person feels about themselves."

Mike nods his head, pursing his lips. He needs to find a way to get the group invested in the importance of self-esteem. Sharon, feeling like she's being targeted, that her insecurities must be transparent asks, "Well, that's just dandy but what does self-esteem have to do with treatment and recovery?"

"Ben," Mike says, trying to drag him out of the land of escapism and into reality. "Would you like to answer Sharon's question?"

"Sure," he says without a fight. "Think about it—if a person naturally feels good about themselves, they're not as likely to entertain the desire to use a mood-altering substance such as alcohol or drugs. If you're happy with the way you are, you don't need a substance to alter it."

"Hold up," Charles interrupts, annoyed. "I hear what you're saying. However, I've used mood-altering substances, but my self-esteem is fine. You're insinuating that just because a person uses a substance, they must have low self-esteem."

"Well, if you feel that good about yourself, why would you risk going to jail, prison, neglecting your family, and putting yourself in high-risk situations in order to use?" Julianne jumps in.

"Hey, what the hell is your problem, Pinkie? Have I done something to you that I don't know about? You've been attacking me all day. And I don't have a damn family. You're the one who lost—"

"Whoa," Julianne defends. "I'm sorry. I'm not attacking you. At least, it's not my intention. On the contrary, it's actually because I care enough about yours and my well-being. I'm trying to be honest with you and myself. I didn't mean anything by it."

"Well, I can't speak for the rest of you, but as for me, I have a lot of self-confidence," Pete interjects, feeling cocky. The group collectively rolls their eyes. "Many of you might not know this but I was promoted by my company two weeks before I entered into treatment and with these two hands I can almost build anything." He looks at his hands as though they'd built the pyramids.

Terry is the first to confront him. "Yeah, we know. You're amazing; you're awesome. You've made sure to tell all of us more than once," she says sarcastically. "But I hope you know there's a difference between *self-confidence* and self-esteem."

"Oh, really?" Charles says, defending Pete. "Why don't you enlighten us."

"Okay," Terry answers, sitting up straight in her chair. Mike, although apprehensive as to where this conversation is going, is glad that his group is pulling itself out of the silent funk.

"Self-confidence," Terry starts, "is your competence to achieve something, like reaching a certain goal; self-*esteem* is how you feel about yourself as a human being."

"Good job," Mike says to Terry. "And to all of you that asked questions and gave feedback, for those of you who would like to take notes on this lecture please feel free." Mike opens his notebook and begins his lecture on self-esteem. Most of the clients began to write down notes on the topic.

BUILDING SELF-ESTEEM

What is self-esteem? Self-esteem is a judgment of how you perceive yourself.

What is self-confidence? Self-confidence is the ability to believe in yourself and to believe you have the ability to achieve or accomplish a goal or task.

Is it possible to have low self-esteem about self, yet be self-confident? Absolutely!

Example: Farmer John was very confident in getting his crops to produce. However, Farmer John felt worthless as a husband and father. This no doubt increased his feeling of inadequacy.

Often self-esteem dictates our behaviors and therefore, our outcome.

Example: Billy Gates thought he was a prepared, senior quarterback for his high school football team. He felt well prepared. He perceived himself as being prepared. He played on that cool, homecoming night as a well-prepared player and by the end of the game, he was pleased with his performance.

Example: Tommy Six thought he wasn't smart enough to keep up with his advanced chemistry class in college. He felt like an outcast. He perceived himself as being a dummy. He then began to neglect his class time and study time, which obviously affected his performance. By the end of the semester, he wasn't pleased with his grade and failed the course. Low self-esteem leads to self-defeating behaviors, and those self-defeating behaviors lead to negative outcomes.

How does alcohol abuse or chemical dependency affect your self-esteem?

It doesn't, although people oftentimes use alcohol and drugs with false hopes that these substances will make them feel better. Sometimes these products, along with impulsive, addictive, and other self-defeating behaviors can be temporarily perceived as productive. Remember, self-esteem is how you feel about yourself. So it doesn't matter what you do to alter your senses and feelings because ultimately, people, places, and things fade or wear off, and once again, you are stuck with yourself. That's why you will not find a single person who abuses alcohol, drugs, or another human being with a positive self-esteem. Think about it: if you feel good about yourself, why would you want to change how you feel by adding a mood-altering substance to your body and mind? Or why would you have the need to downplay another person instead of building that person up?

Another example may help you understand more about self-esteem: It would sound a little silly to go to the dope dealer or bootlegger at two or three o'clock in the morning and say, "Dope, man. Give me some of that stuff that makes me feel how I feel, because I feel wonderful about myself." That sounds silly because why would anyone with high self-esteem put themselves or their family in harm's way by turning to alcohol, drugs, unhealthy relationships, or other impulsive or self-defeating behaviors?

HOW TO BUILD SELF-ESTEEM

Get familiar with your value system.

Values. *What does that word mean?*

Values represent what is important to you. Ideally, if something is important to you, you will take care of it, Right?

For Example:
  Family
  Children
  Health
  Life
  Freedom
  Home
  Job

Be careful not to contradict yourself. How many times have you said that you value something, only to put alcohol, drugs, or self-defeating behaviors above your words?

Get familiar with setting goals.

It is important to set a goal because it gives you something to measure your success by. Is this goal right for me? Too often goals are set for other people.

Be specific when setting goals. Don't say, "I think I'll go back to school and study for a new career." Instead say, "I'm going back to school to study *accounting* for a new career."

Is the goal reasonable? Remember, it doesn't matter how small or large the goal is, as long as it's realistic to you.

Self-care

When building self-esteem, it is important to take care of your body (temple):

Exercise regularly. Consult your physician and discuss a workout plan.

Healthy Eating Habits

Get to know your foods and the dos and don'ts that will help you to a healthier lifestyle.

Proper Hygiene

Nurture yourself daily by taking the necessary steps to maintain your hygiene.

Spirituality

Spirituality plays a major part in building self-esteem. Spirituality is a feeling of calmness and peace. A person doesn't have to be religious to achieve spirituality.

Assertiveness

Allows one to be sure of self: bold when dealing with others.

Honesty

Allows one to be upright and sincere with self and others.

Integrity

Allows one the quality of trustworthiness and being complete.

Sobriety

Abstinence is the ability to be alcohol-free and drug-free. It is "Mission Impossible" to be drunk or high and clean and sober at the same time.

Involvement

It is important to stay involved with family, friends, and positive community activities rather than isolating and keeping your good fortunes that are due to sobriety all to yourself.

Acceptance

Admitting the truth when you drink or get high, and about how others and you are affected. Acceptance is the truth for each of you.

The opposite of acceptance is denial. Denial may seem to be the alcohol or drug user's good friend, because denial can allow a person to do many things:

1. Allows the alcohol or drug user to assign blame. As long as there is someone or something to blame, the user may not move into acceptance.
2. Allows the alcohol or drug user to create excuses for why they do as they do.
3. Allows the alcohol or drug user to minimize their situation—makes it seem less severe or not as bad as it truly is.
4. Allows the alcohol or drug user to justify their feelings and behaviors.

Remember, by getting familiar with your own value system and starting to live by it, you will increase your self-esteem.

We are out of time. Any questions? If not, let us close with, "Hope for a Better Day."

PRECIOUS SOULS

Counselor Mike's therapeutic work is getting through to Sharon. She is willing to take a risk and express her change of heart with another peer in the clients' lounge.

"Hey, Ben. Do you have a moment?" Sharon asks, taking a seat in front of him. Ben is working on a crossword puzzle and is hesitant to speak with her. "I really need to talk to you," she says, trying again.

"Sure," he says, placing his magazine on the table. "What's up? You okay?"

"Yeah," she says, staring at the floor. She feels ashamed, but has to get it out. "But anyway, my counselor, Mike asked me to apologize to you for calling you a derogatory name."

"You mean for calling me a faggot?" he asks, forcing her to confront her damaging behavior.

"Yeah. And actually, *I* want to apologize."

Ben feels sorry for her. He realizes how much it must have taken for her to apologize to him. "You know what, friend girl, don't even trip over it. I've been called worse. Thank you though. I appreciate the apology."

Sharon smiles, finally lifting her head from the ground. It's hard for her to believe he let her off the hook so easily. Had the shoe been on the other foot, she's not sure she would have been as forgiving. "Yeah, I can imagine, Ben. Still, it wasn't right for me to be rude like that to you."

"Sharon, please don't beat yourself up. Sometimes we all say and do things that we come to regret later." Ben scoots up to the edge of his chair and takes her hand. Although she can't believe a homosexual is holding her hand, his touch comforts her.

"You know, Ben, some of the people I know would have a major problem with you and I havin' a civil conversation such as this."

"Hmm," Ben thinks about it. "Well, how do you feel about it?"

"Honestly, Ben, I'm not sure how I feel." She doesn't want to admit how she feels. It goes against everything she's ever learned. Everything she's ever heard from the people she loves, the people who love her have told her what she is doing is wrong, but she doesn't feel that way. It's very confusing. She looks into Ben's eyes and she doesn't see a faggot. She sees a young man who struggles, who suffers just as she does; she sees a man who has never hurt her and can't imagine him hurting anyone. "However, I am *sure* that I would like to stop having so much anger toward other people."

"So, how have you been working on your anger issues toward others?"

"Counselor Mike . . . he's said some things to me, which, I don't know how he has done it, has gotten me to explore inside myself. He gave me exercise material on feelings and he encourages me, which some days I can't believe considering how I've treated him, but they help me to feel my own feelings and they help me identify the ones that feel good and the ones that feel bad."

"That sounds like a workable treatment plan," Ben replies. "As for me Sharon, the therapeutic groups and lectures have really helped me. For the first time that I can remember in my life, I feel okay in my own skin."

"That's real nice, Ben. We've been lying to ourselves for years, haven't we? We are not misfits or victims to society, but precious souls. At least, that's what I've been reading."

"And you're right," Ben answers.

"Well, Ben, I'm glad you were strong enough to accept my apology. I really do think you are beautiful." The two embrace and Sharon can't help but laugh a little bit. What would her parents think if they could see her now? They pull away from each other and Sharon can see the clock behind Ben.

"Ooh, sorry to cut our conversation short," she says, getting to her feet, "but you know how everything is on a schedule 'round here. I need to start heading toward my women's group so I won't be late again. Thanks, Ben, for listening to me. I guess I'll catch up to you later?"

"You bet," Ben replies with a smile. "I'll talk with you later."

IT'S TIME TO GET HONEST

Charles is finally realizing that he doesn't have to be Billy Badass all the time. The men are coming in to the clients' lounge after group therapy and begin a conversation. (Trust God and God will provide. His grace may not be how we think it should be or how we want it to be, but He will provide.) Read on and see how He provides Charles with a support team.

"Hey, Charles. You did good work in the therapy group today," Steve says, leaning up against the counter as Charles makes his coffee. "You really shared your feelings. That took courage, man. How do you feel?"

"Honestly, I still can't believe I did that," Charles replies, stirring his coffee. "I usually try to keep that kind of stuff to myself, but once I started, and I saw how the group responded, I knew it would be all right."

"I remember the first time I opened up in group," Pazmate interrupts, putting his phone away into his coat pocket.

"Oh, yeah? Was it tough?" Charles asks.

"As a matter of fact, I had a lot of mixed feelings. I didn't know if I was coming or going, but once I got all the garbage that I've been carrying around for years out, I felt better." Charles pours an extra cup of coffee for Pazmate and they collect together around the coffee table.

"You still haven't answered Steve's question," Marty says joining the group. "How do you feel about it?"

"I feel good," he replies. "I feel real good. I gotta admit, I'm a little shaky," Charles says, holding out his hand so the others can see it tremor.

"I'm glad you decided to open up. We're not here to hurt or judge you; we're all here trying to get better."

"As it turns out," Charles responds with a smile.

"Marty is right," Steve says. "We all remember what our lives were like when we were using."

Charles nods, taking a moment to remember what his life was like only a few short months ago. He looks at Pete who hasn't had much to say recently and who has spent most of his time staring at his lap. "You haven't said much, Pete. What's on your mind, brotha?"

Pete shrugs. He's conflicted about how he feels. He has spent so much of his time bottling himself up because he thought he always needed to be the man in all situations and now he's had to reconsider what it really means to be one. "I didn't realize how angry I was until I started to look at myself and others." He looks up and around at his peers and realizing that he actually has their full attention, continues on. "Taking a risk and sharing how I really feel during the therapeutic groups and opening up to my counselor, I actually look toward the future. I never had that. I was always too pre-occupied with . . . I don't even know anymore."

The group collects around Pete to show their support. Pazmate reaches into his pocket and turns off his cell phone and says,

"This recovery stuff isn't as bad as I made it out to be, as much as I hate to admit it. It's not like I ever heard of anyone going to jail, losing their families or jobs because they were too clean and sober."

"I guess Pazmate is right, Pete," Charles chides in. "I had it in my head that only squares were clean, know what I mean? I thought being clean meant throwing away a fun life. I'd see people who were sober and I'd think that their lives had to be boring."

"Hell, I used to think that if I came to treatment, the counselors would brainwash me!" Pete adds.

"That's funny, because that is exactly what Charles and I discussed some weeks ago," Marty adds. "But I realized that even if it took brainwashing for me to live a happy joyous life, I hoped these counselors would brainwash the hell out of me!"

"Turns out treatment and learning the dangers and consequences of substance abuse were good for me," Charles says. "Or so it seems. Man, didn't see that one comin'."

"Why do you use the word, 'seems'?" Pazmate asks. "Either it has or has not been good for you."

"Pazmate is right, Charles," Steve adds. "Should we review what life was like *before* treatment?" he says, sarcastically.

"Okay! Okay!" Charles says, waving his hands above his head. "I admit it, coming to treatment has been beneficial for me. You happy?"

Marty laughs, saying, "I don't know about Steve, but I've been happy for a while. Are you happy? Happy? Happy?" he mocks.

"Yeah, yeah, yeah. I'm happy," Charles replies. "Can't you see my joy?"

"Good. We're all happy. On that happy note, it's getting late and I need to go work on my discharge plan," Pete says, collecting his things and heading for the exit.

"See ya," the group says as Pete heads out the door.

"Well, I hate to bail on you cats," Charles says after a moment of silence, "but I have kitchen detail." Charles gets up from his chair. "I'll catch up to you guys later."

"Okay. See ya," they reply.

WHAT IS THE GOOD STUFF?

Skeety, always a beautiful woman, comes into work looking more elegant than usual. Meeting with the women at Mission Impossible Counseling to have a discussion with the women alone has inspired her to look her best.

"Okay, ladies," Skeety says, daintily taking her place in her chair. "Today our topic is going to be on What is *The Good Stuff?*"

"The good stuff?" Minnie asks. "I don't even know what that looks like."

The group of women chuckle, which displeases Skeety. "Come on, ladies, let's focus." Because Minnie felt the need to distract the other girls from the conversation, Skeety addresses her. "Well, Minnie, why don't you tell me and the other ladies what your ideal of the good stuff is." Minnie takes a moment to think about it, though, that she's been asked, the answer is much simpler than she thought.

"My idea of the good stuff," she says, with a smile directed at the floor, "is having someone love me just for who I am and don't keep throwing my past up in my face." Minnie can't help but wonder if there is a person alive who will truly love her like that. She starts gnawing at her short, stubby fingernails to avoid talking about it further.

"Very good, Minnie. What does the good stuff mean to you, Julianne?"

Julianne immediately thinks of her children. "For me, the good stuff means having my children back and never losing them again. I don't want my reckless life to take them from me ever again."

"Terry?" the counselor asks, motioning to Terry.

"The good stuff?"

Skeety nods.

"To me—it's accepting my past and facing the future with hope and enthusiasm. I can't remember the last time I felt hopeful."

"Would you mind sharing with the group, Sharon?"

Sharon smiles.

"The good stuff is taking responsibility for my actions and feelings. I'm a little tired of worrying about everyone else all the time. I've come to realize that they don't want it or need it and frankly, it's exhausting." She smiles.

"Good job, ladies. For the next exercise, remember to answer the question as honestly as possible. Julianne, if you knew you only had twenty-four hours left to live, who would you try to be with and what would you do?"

"I would be with my children holding them." Julianne takes a moment to picture her children wrapped up in her arms, laughing and smiling. Maybe they'd be as glad to see her as she would be to see them. "I'd talk to them, ya know? Nothing fantastic or heroic. I'd just make sure they knew how much I really love them. Ask them about their day at school, make popsicles, I don't know, anything."

"How would you spend your time, Terry?"

"I would spend my time with homeless people, encouraging them that there is hope for a better life. Hell, I might even start dating again."

The girls laugh and assure her that any man in her future is in big trouble and they'd be happy to help.

"Minnie, with only twenty-four hours left in your life, what would you do?"

"I'd spend it with my brother and sister. We'd sit on the porch and reminisce. Maybe spend some time talking about Mom. Talk about everything she taught us—everything she gave us." Minnie misses her aunt's front porch. She misses the spot on the railing that faces the front yard, where she'd sit on top of it and bang the back of her ankles against the banister as she'd sip her mom's juice and listen to the neighborhood children walk home from school. She could hear her mom and aunt discussing how the neighborhood had gone to hell.

"Sharon, how 'bout you?"

"I guess I'd spend it with my family too. I'd like to tell them about all the wonderful things I've learned here so they'd know that *this* time, I'm better. That finally, they have their daughter back." But she wondered if they'd get the Sharon they'd want. She's sober, but what about her other changes? She tried to picture what her parents would do if she came home with a Mexican boyfriend or a gay friend. She couldn't help but smile to herself, just a little bit.

"For our next exercise, let's talk about what you would *not* want to do if you knew you only had twenty-four hours to live. We'll start with you, Terry."

Terry pictures her life before treatment. The nights she spent with her cheek rested on the bowl of the toilet, digging through the cupboards, throwing bottles away, looking for the one that had enough in it to get her through the day until she could make it to the store. "Not drunk," she offers, ready to say goodbye to spending money she didn't have to pay for cheap liquor. "I'm just tired of it."

"Fantastic," Skeety says. "Straight, simple, to the point, and fantastic. As for you, Julianne?"

Julianne thinks about being back in her apartment. Struggling to get to work on time and tripping over toys belonging to children who are no longer there. Her latest relationship snoring wildly, alcohol on his breath as she stares at the small, empty beds. "Being without my children is the saddest thing I can think of. I don't want that."

"What would you not like, Sharon?"

Sharon shakes her head, ashamed of her own behavior and trying to punish herself as though she were a disobedient child. "Going back to my old behaviors and thoughts, which leads me to negative consequences and I would not like to spend my last twenty-four hours of life that away. I'm finished with it. I'm serious, if I knew I had only twenty-four more hours of life on this Earth, would I seriously waste it on hating or judging other people? Of course not. That's stupid. I can't believe I've wasted as much time as I have on it."

Skeety is trying to hide it, but she's excited, and proud. She can't help but feel a little self-satisfaction at the girls' progress.

"How about you, Minnie?"

"Not doin' nothin'. That's for sure. I wanna be busy, ya know. Livin' my life to the fullest. Real kind of stuff, ya know?"

"Good job, ladies. You all did good work on this exercise. I noticed some of you becoming emotional. There's nothing wrong with that because recovery is about recovering the feelings that have been hidden away, neglected. Try to remember: one of the first things that comes back once you begin to recover is buried feelings. Does anyone have any questions before we start the lecture on Level I, II, and III? No?"

LEVEL I, II AND III
THE POWER OF CHANGE:
A DISCUSSION ACTIVITY

Skeety writes, "Levels I, II, and III" on the board.

Level I is written on the upper left side of the board.

Level II is written on the lower right side of the board.

Level III is written on the upper right side of the board.

Below *Level III,* she writes, "*Recovery.*" Asking the group if they think the discussion of recovery is the ideal place to begin treatment.

The group takes a few minutes to share their thoughts on the question. She shares with the group that discussing recovery isn't always the best place to start. Why not? Skeety explains to the group why one should not start with recovery:

1. Some clients may feel they don't have a problem with addiction, and if they don't have a problem with addiction, they have no need to discuss it.
2. Some clients may feel that they have a problem with addiction but do not want to do anything about it.

So instead of starting on Level III, it may be more appropriate to begin on Level I.

Level I: The Self-Contract

She explains that a *contract* is an agreement between two or more people or parties. A *self-contract* is an agreement made with oneself. This level is the *need*. This level gives a clear indication of whether a client needs to go to the next level. Start Level I by writing on the board:

Negative   *Positive*

She explains to the clients that there are some common statements alcohol and drug users say when describing their self-contracts.

Negative	Positive
I will drink	I won't drive
I will use	I will limit my usage
I will drink	only at home
I will use	but not at home
I will drink	I will not fight with spouse
I will use	I won't go to jail
I will drink	It will not interfere with work
I will use	I will pay bills
I will drink	I won't stay out too late
I will use	I will not neglect responsibilities
I will drink	I won't let it interfere with my family

Skeety asks the clients if they can identify with any of the examples on the board and share their own examples.

The clients know that if they have failed at a single deed on their self-contract, it is an indication that a need for recovery is a possibility.

She tells the clients a self-contract is about being honest and real. What is on most self-contracts are promises and words they've told themselves many times before.

For example: How many times have you told yourself, "When I use, I will do this or I won't do that," though eventually, you find yourself going against your words?

Level II: Having a Desire

This is the "want" level. It gives a clear indication of whether a client *wants* to go to the next level.

Skeety asks the clients to answer the question: "How will I benefit by not using?"

She explains to the clients that there are some common statements alcohol and drug users say before they are asked how they will benefit:

I won't get a DUI
I will have better family relationships
I will be less likely to have legal problems
I will be more responsible
I will probably be home more
I will have a better work relationship
I will have better health
I will be more involved with my children
I will manage my finances better
I will have better social relationships

Can you identify with any of the examples on the board and would like to share your own examples?

By understanding and identifying with Level I and Level II, you can then move on to Level III.

Level III: Recovery

This is the working level—the action.

Skeety writes on the board, under *Recovery* the basic H.O.W formula:

Honesty. "How has your usage been problematic for others?"

Open-mindedness. "What part has your usage played in your recent problems?"

Willingness. Describe a treatment plan to improve your situation.

She writes, *"Change"* on the board and asks, "What must come first before any change can begin?"

Answer: There must be a reason before any change occurs. Why do I want to change? What is the reason?

She continues, "If there's a good reason to change. Does that mean that change will automatically occur?"

Answer: No. You may have the best intentions in the world for change and change may not occur.

Reason + Motivation = Change

When a reason is identified, you must then be motivated to do whatever is in your power to make change occur.

Examples of some possible reasons for change:
    Better health
    Better family relationships
    Better self-esteem
    Better parenting
    Better social involvement
    Better financial status
    Better job performance
    Better chance to obtain freedom

Once you have found a reason to change, you must then be motivated to change.

So before you even begin to discuss recovery, sometimes you first need to be clear on your *needs* and *wants*.

"That was deep, Skeety," Sharon says, smiling.

"I agree," Skeety replies. "And I'm sorry we can't elaborate more on this topic but we have run over our group time. Ladies, will you all please join me in closing this group with 'Hope for a Better Day.'"

SMOKE-FREE IN MAROON VILLAGE

Shylisa
Pardon me, Ms. Kool, but we're trying to find out what's good about smoking. Do you think you can help us?

Ms. Kool
Well, smoking can lead to a fast death if you don't want to live as long. Smokers are three times more likely to die of heart disease and lung cancer. Also, if you are one of those people who don't like to brush, smoking will accommodate you, because you are more likely to have gum disease and lose teeth.

Brendon
Thanks, Ms. Kool, but that's not exactly the information we're looking for.

Ms. Kool
How about this: once you become addicted to nicotine, tobacco takes control of your life. Nicotine will influence when, where, and how often you need to smoke. And the average smoker spends thousands of dollars on cigarettes each year.

Brendon
That's just not the answers we're looking for, Ms. Kool. But thanks anyway. Bye now.

Ms. Kool

I'm sorry I wasn't very helpful to you, but maybe the Marlboro Man could be more of assistance. And if you hurry, you could catch up to him now enjoying a smoke with a group of people on smoke break.

(A group of people is gathered together smoking and coughing, as the Marlboro Man walks away).

Shylisa
There he is. I see him.

Brendon
Where?

Shylisa
He's leaving that group of people standing over there coughing.

Brendon
Oh yeah, I see him. Let's go catch up.

(The two friends continue on their journey toward the Marlboro Man.)

Shylisa
Marlboro Man! Marlboro Man! Sorry to burn your butt, but could you please explain the benefit of smoking to us?

Marlboro Man
Well for one, it gives you a chance to be one of the cool people that rarely excel in academia and sports. Smoking cigarettes is a very expensive habit that affects your health in many ways. However, you must understand one thing: it's much easier to quit school and sports, but it's hard to quit smoking.

Brendon
Thanks, Marlboro Man. We gotta go now. Hope not to see you later.

(The two friends start to walk away.)

Marlboro Man

Hang on, youngsters. You also need to know your body needs oxygen. When you inhale, fresh air travels to your lungs. In your lungs, oxygen enters the bloodstream and is carried throughout your body.

Shylisa

Wow! I never knew how much work our
lungs do throughout our bodies.

Brendon

That's interesting information, but what does
that have to do with cigarette smoking?

Marlboro Man

When people smoke, they breathe in harmful chemicals, including tar, a thick black material that sticks to their lungs and is suspected to cause cancer. They also breathe in carbon monoxide, a poisonous gas that replaces oxygen in the bloodstream. And to further add, they breathe in nicotine, an addictive (habit-forming) drug. What nicotine does is it makes the heart work faster, and in large doses, it can even be fatal!

Brendon

Man! This is deep. Smoking is more harmful than I ever imagined.

Shylisa

Yeah, really. I think you've said enough, Marlboro Man. Thanks. Bye.

(The two friends leave Marlboro Man and continue walking. Moments later the two friends are intercepted by the Dope Man.)

Dope Man

Hello, friends. You two look a little stressed. How about a sack of this good stuff? *(Shaking a bag of drugs in front of them)*

Brendon
Sorry, we're not falling for that! We have better
things to do with our lives than drugs.

Dope Man
Like what? Stay in high school, get good grades then go to
college? And then return back to the Maroon Villege with more
knowledge that will benefit and strengthen our people?

Shylisa
Yep! You've got that right.

Dope Man
Well, while you two champions are doing well in school,
I'm out here making a big dollar by doing my thing!

Brendon
Maybe you are, but you are also hurting the
people in the Maroon Village.

Dope Man
And your point is?

Shylisa
Only that you might *think* you're living large, but the way you
are living is not a part of the Maroon people traditions.

Brendon
That's right. Doing illegal drugs is not part of our heritage.

Shylisa
Come on, Brendon. Jump a lake, he doesn't seem to be feeling us.

Brendon
Bet! Let's bounce.

(The two friends leave the Dope Man standing there pondering on the science they just dropped on him.)

Shylisa
Wait a minute, Brendon, he is our people.

Brendon
True dat. Come on, girl. Let's do what's right.

(After taking four steps forward, the two friends turn around and walk back to the Dope Man and give him a brochure on the dangers of drugs, and continue on their way. Moments later, they are intercepted by Grandma Mozell sitting by the pavilion tree.)

Shylisa
Hi, Grandma Mozell. Why are you sitting all by your lonesome on such a wonderful blue-sky day?

Grandma Mozell
I'm not alone at all. I have the Great Spirit with me.

Brendon
Grandma Mozell, how do you manage to stay so spiritual all the time? I mean, you are so strong and your faith seems to reach eternity.

Grandma Mozell
My, my, my! Youngsters, I'm not strong at all, but the Great Spirit is. And with the Great Spirit, all things are possible.

Shylisa
Grandma Mozell, do you think it's wrong to smoke cigarettes?

Grandma Mozell
Why are you asking such a thing?

Shylisa

I just want to know.

Grandma Mozell

Well, I can't decide for anyone what's right and what's wrong: that is between the Great Spirit and them. But I can share with others the experiences I had with cigarettes when I used to smoke.

Brendon

Grandma Mozell! Shut your mouth! Are you telling me you used to smoke cigarettes?

Grandma Mozell

Yes, my little handsome knight. As a matter of fact, I used to smoke two packs a day.

Shylisa

Why did you quit?

Grandma Mozell

My story goes like this. One day I was at my parent's house visiting and enjoying a thankful moment, talking with my father on the back deck. During this time, my mother was in the kitchen cooking. All of a sudden the house began to fill up with smoke. My mother called me into the kitchen and told me to go stand in the smoke.

Brendon

Why? Didn't she notice how smoky the house was?

Grandma Mozell

Of course, she did. When I mentioned to her how unhealthy it was to breathe in all the smoke that was coming from the stove, she kindly reminded me that I breathe in unhealthy smoke with every cigarette I inhale.

Shylisa
Your mother was a very wise woman.

Grandma Mozell
That she was, and from that lesson, I'd never smoked cigarettes again.

Brendon
Grandma Mozell, the Great Spirit is good.

Grandma Mozell
All the time, the Great Spirit is good.

Shylisa
Grandma Mozell, we still have a few decisions we have to make for ourselves. Thanks for the wisdom. We'll talk to you later. You have a blessed day.

Grandma Mozell
Thank you, child. And you two youngsters have a blessed day also. Bye now and remember to ask Great Spirit to be your guide in the paths you take.

(The two friends wave goodbye to Grandma Mozell and continue on their journey.)

Shylisa
You know, Brendon, I'm glad my mom almost caught me smoking last night. Because now I know it's just not worth the trouble. And if I have to smoke to be on a losing team, I'd rather be smoke-free and be a single winner.

Brendon
I hear you talkin'. Today let's make a vow to stay strong, smart, and beautiful, the Maroon Tribe way, and smoking cigarettes is not part of our traditional way.

Shylisa
True dat.

Brendon
So girl, let's just: shake, shake, shake, shake, shake, shake, shake our butts, shake our butts.
(Repeat. As they throw down their cigarettes while stomping them into the ground and singing and doing the shake dance.)

Shylisa
Well, Brendon, I gotta bounce. I still need to go visit my cousin Minnie. She's heading to the Mission Impossible Counseling program for substance abuse treatment tomorrow.

Brendon
I forgot all about your cousin going to treatment. I hope she does well and changes that crazy lifestyle of hers around for the better.

Shylisa
Me too. I've heard the counselors there are really good!

Brendon
Okay, Shylisa. I'll get back with you later. Have a great evening.

Shylisa
Bye now. You have a great evening too. Thanks for hanging out with me today.

Brendon
No problem. That's what friends are for.

CHAPTER 4

18 AND LIFE TO GO

People raised in functional or dysfunctional homes typically have a tendency to play out the family role and view the world through the eyes of the people most important and most influential in their lives. People raised within functional families generally learn from an early age how to govern their behaviors and are acceptable to constructive criticism as they can recognize inappropriate behaviors. People raised within dysfunctional families generally learn from an early age to blame others for their behaviors and are not acceptable to constructive criticism as they recognize inappropriate behaviors. Typically families have values; what's important here is, once becoming an adult, one has to discover which family value has or hasn't been working.

1. Did your parents support and encourage you to do well in school?
2. Did your parents support and encourage you to be involved with sports, music, drama, church, and such?
3. Did your parents protect you physically and emotionally from outside predators?

HE DOESN'T SEEM RIGHT

Counselor Mike isn't dressing as well as he used to. He twitches like he's on drugs, appears irritable, and doesn't want to talk to his colleagues.

"Hi, Mike! How is your day thus far?" Skeety asks, entering the commons with Inky.

"Oh, hey guys. My day is going well so far. Yours?"

"It's goin' well. Thanks for asking. Hey," Skeety continues trying to get Mike's attention. He is reluctant to raise his head from the table which is covered in paperwork. "Some of the staff are going to Snappy's for lunch. Would you like to join us?"

"Thanks for the offer," he replies, not taking his head away from a form in his hand, ". . . but no thanks. I have so much work to do around here. I think it's best if I skip lunch today and catch up on some of my paperwork."

"Mike, are you doing okay?" Inky asks because of the prodding look Skeety is giving him. "You seem to be isolating."

"What?" Mike asks and looks up for only a second. Inky looks at Skeety for an escape, but she encourages him forward. "You've been spending a lot of time in your office lately."

"Come on, guys," Mike says with a sigh. "I'm very busy." Mike puts his paper down and takes the time to wipe the stress off of his face. "Maybe I need a vacation."

"You—take time away from work?" Skeety asks, laughing and shocked. "That would be the day. Could you imagine Mike taking time off of work?" she asks Inky.

"Not even a little," he replies. "I don't know how you do it, Mike. I think you must be a machine."

Mike scoffs. "No, Inky. I'm just a man with 'super' in front!" he says, puffing out his chest.

"Are you sure you're doing alright, Mike?" Skeety says, pushing the issue. She sits down in front of Mike to let him know he has a friend. "You seem like you have lost a lot of weight in the last couple of months."

"I'm fine," Mike says more adamantly. "There's no need to keep worrying yourself about me." Mike grips his paper tightly and Skeety takes the hint.

"Okay," she says, defeated. "If you say so." Skeety gets up and takes her place back next to Inky. Inky, taking one more chance on Mike opening up says, "Before I forget, Sharon was looking for you earlier."

Mike nods. "Thanks for letting me know. She has made a lot of progress from the time she entered treatment."

"Okay, Mike," Skeety says, giving Mike one last chance for socialization. "Being that you turned down Inky and my invitation to join us for lunch, would you like for us to order you something to eat while we're at Snappy's?"

"No. I think I'll decline. I had a pretty big breakfast this morning. I don't think I can eat another bite."

"Huh," Inky says, looking at his coconspirator. "I wonder where it all went. Can you see it anywhere?" he asks Skeety, looking under the table, trying to make a joke that Mike doesn't take the time to acknowledge.

"I can't see it either, Inky. Maybe he's hiding that big meal somewhere," Skeety says looking at Mike as though he were stashing a hamburger in his clothes.

"Ha ha," Mike says, waving them away. "With that, that's my cue to go to my office and get to work. You two counselors have a great lunch," Mike says, shuffling his work into a messy pile and scooping it up in his arms. "Later."

"Bye, Mike," the two call back, but he is already halfway down the hall. Now that they're left alone, Skeety looks at Inky and says, "I really think something is wrong with him. He's been acting very strange lately."

"I know what you mean," Inky replies, not having an answer to the problem. "He barely even talks to me anymore. Something isn't right."

HOPE FOR A BETTER DAY

As Sharon walks into Counselor Mike's office, she thinks back to her first day of treatment, when she waited for him to arrive. The pictures on the wall that she once thought were dreadful, she now admires. As she nears Counselor Mike sitting behind his desk, he welcomes her warmly.

"Sharon, how are you doing? Grab a seat. I was told by Inky you were looking for me earlier. How can I assist you?"

Taking a deep breath and her seat she says, "I just wanted to let you know I've completed all of my assignments, and tomorrow when I discharge, I feel I'm ready to live life on life terms."

"Great news, Sharon! I think you'll do well back in your community." Sharon smiles at his praise. "But remember," he continues, "it's not always going to be easy. You will be confronted with many obstacles and challenges."

"I know," she says looking out the window. "I also know my attitude wasn't very good when I first arrived here." Sharon is looking for a way to forgive herself and hopes Mike will be able to as well. She tucks her hands between her legs and staring at her thumbs, says, "I wanna thank you for allowing me to grow at my own pace."

With a nod of Mike's head, Sharon knows she's forgiven. Mike says, "You're welcome, Sharon. I'm proud of you. It takes much courage to explore new ideas and visions while here in treatment and you have made major progress."

"I didn't want to be here at first, but when you encouraged me to take responsibility and look at my own issues, I finally, for the first time in my life, am able to get honest about what is going on inside of me."

"So share with me," Mike says, comforting his client for probably the last time, "when you get back to your community, what are some of the goals you've set for yourself in order to support your recovery?"

"I'm gonna attend twelve-step meetings, because I have proven to myself for years I can't do it alone. But most importantly, I need to work on a recovery program."

"How difficult do you think it's going to be for you when your associates begin to realize you have a new attitude about people, places, and things?"

Sharon has a lost and scared look on her face. What was once a fence keeping her against her will had become arms holding her, protecting her from everything on the other side of it. "You mean my White Knight family, don't you?" Mike nods. "How will they react towards me after they find out I have different views now?" She takes a moment to answer his question. "To tell you the truth, I don't know how I'm going to handle that situation."

"Do you feel as if your life may be in danger? I need you to be honest with me," Mike says, leaning forward over his desk.

"Right now, all I can think about is living one day at a time."

"Well, with that being said, and with the haphazard, confident look on your face, it seems to me you've invested in your treatment well, Sharon."

"Thanks to you and the program," Sharon says, hoping the compliment to him means as much to Mike as it does to her to say it. "Counselor Mike, I feel I have a chance to live a joyous, happy life and I have hope for a better day."

Mike smiles and jokingly waves his finger at her. "Remember young lady: you create your own happiness. That is one responsibility you cannot hand over to anyone else."

Sharon smiles. "I'm not perfect, but I am beginning to understand. Thanks for everything. I guess I'll see ya. I still need to finish packing so I'll be ready for discharge tomorrow."

"Good luck to you, Sharon. It is a pleasure knowing you." Mike stands up and extends his hand over his desk. Sharon welcomes his gesture by shaking the hand of the counselor she once hated and exits his office.

FAMILY REUNION

Ben spent family day with his parents. His friends are trying to comfort and encourage him to keep smiling, keep shining, and know he can always count on them, for sure, because that's what friends are for.

"So, how was it, Ben? Don't keep us in suspense," Terry says getting up from her chair and approaching her gay friend.

"He said he loves me, Terry. He loves me!" Ben says with tears in his eyes. Terry gives him a big hug and says, "That's awesome! You were worried for nothing." Terry, having no children of her own, has taken Ben under her wing.

"And my mom. She loves me too!"

The rest of the group, hearing the good news, all stand up and join Ben and Terry in their excitement.

"Well, how is your pops feeling?" Minnie asks.

"He says he's doing okay, but he didn't look so well."

"I'm sorry, Ben," Terry says wishing Minnie hadn't brought it up. She gives Minnie a dirty look.

"It's not your fault," Ben says, grabbing a cup of celebratory coffee. "I guess this happy family reunion also turned out to be a sad one."

"I'm sorry," Minnie says, rubbing Ben's shoulder. "I didn't mean to bring you down by asking you about your pops."

"It's not you, Minnie," Ben says. "Thank you for your consideration."

"What about your mom, how is she holding up?" Terry asks, looking for an immediate change of subject.

"My mom? She's always been tough," Ben says, reflecting on his mother. She won't let Dad see how scared and sad she is. My mom has always been strong as a brick."

"So what did you and your pops talk about? Is he still having a hard time dealing with you being gay?" Minnie asks.

"He'll never agree with it, but he's forgiven me. He said he did about three years ago. He just didn't know how to say it."

"That's great, Ben!" Terry says, offering up a toast.

"Yes, I know," Ben says like a little kid. "And guess what?" he says, looking at Minnie.

"What?"

"My parents want me to move in with them, so I can help Mom around the house and help her take care of Dad."

"See, Ben? Your family does love you," Terry says, trying once again to offer a toast.

"You're so right. Thanks. You guys really are like family to me."

"Oh, no, watch out. Ben's startin' that mushy stuff again," Minnie says, laughing.

"No, I really mean it," Ben interjects. "You are like my own family. I love you guys."

Minnie smiles bashfully, but Terry's eyes fill up with tears. This is the closest thing she's had to a family in, she can't remember how long. A part of her doesn't want to leave. She doesn't want them in her group to leave. And though she knows that can't happen, she's going to miss them. On the other hand, she realizes that even though she's too old to have children, she can still start a little family of her own.

"We know you're sincere, Ben," Terry says, defending Ben's vulnerability. "I want you to know you have also been here for us. Isn't that right, Minnie?" Terry says, elbowing Minnie in the side.

"Yeah, yeah, yeah, it's true," Minnie says pretending to hate defeat. "I'm just glad you and your pops made up."

"Me too," Terry says.

"Thanks, you guys. When I leave here, I'm really going to miss you."

"Well, if you ever feel brave enough," Minnie says, raising her eyebrow, "you know where to find me. 112 W. Elm Street. Holla at me."

"And you have my phone number," Terry says. "Give me a call sometime."

"I will."

IT'S CALLED BIPOLAR

Pazmate is using the skills that he has learned while in treatment. Julianne appears confused and hurt, but is thankful to have discovered that there are genuine people in this world she can lean on when times are tough.

"Has anyone seen Julianne?" Pazmate asks coming into the clients' lounge.

"Yeah," Pete replies, turning around in his seat. I had seen her working on her assignment at the outside worktable."

"Thanks, Pete," Pazmate replies, rushing out of the room.

Walking out into the treatment center's courtyard, Pazmate sees Julianne sitting at a table with her head down, focusing on her worksheet. She's twirling her hair with her left hand and chewing her pencil with the help of her right.

"Hey," Pazmate barks, startling Julianne. "You're on dishwashing detail this week! You forget?"

"Wow. I'm on dishes detail, so—are you on 'my father' detail?" she snaps back, returning to her work as though his insult hasn't affected her.

"No," he says, straddling the bench across from her, "but I am the client's president this week and one of my responsibilities as president is to remind people of their chores."

"Wow, so you're like the hall monitor, huh? So Mr. Rich Guy, sounds like you really enjoy the power," she says, starting a daisy doodle in the margin of her worksheet.

"What's gotten into you?" he asks with a gnarled look on his face. "This morning you were one of the most pleasant people I'd ever met and now it seems like you want to rip my head off. Is this a 'girl' thing?" he asks, calmly, trying to de-escalate the situation. It doesn't work.

Julianne takes offense to the sexist comment and replies, "For your information, Sergeant Pazmate, it's called bipolar disorder and what that means, if your brain can't figure it out, is that my emotions are all out of whack. Half the time I don't know if I'm coming or going."

Pazmate can see Julianne's lip quiver and though he hates letting a woman's tears get the best of him, he can't help but give in. "I'm sorry you have to go through that, Julianne. I thought you were taking medication for that."

"I am," she says looking into the wind, trying to control her tears. "But I really hate it."

"Why? I thought they were supposed to make you feel better."

"That's my point. It's so aggravating," she says, firmly gripping her pencil. "The medicine makes me feel worse."

Pazmate is stumped. He's never been particularly good at comforting women and everything in his past and experience has told him to avoid all confrontation with a weepy woman, but this felt different. He couldn't leave Julianne.

"Have you talked with your primary counselor about your feelings?"

Julianne nods. "She told me to give it more time."

"You know," Pazmate continues, trying to fix Julianne, "you can go straight to the facility doctor and speak with him about the concerns you have."

"Yeah, I know."

Her head is still focused on her worksheet. He takes her hand, so she'll look at him. "So are you?"

"No. I think I'll take my counselor's advice and give the medication a few days."

"Well," Pazmate says, accepting failure, "I hope it starts working for you fast, because I don't know what to expect from you minute to minute."

He hoped his statement would make her laugh, but it only made the tears fall at a more rapid pace.

"I'm so sorry for being so rude to you. You don't deserve it. Forgive me?"

She looks at him, her eyes large and glassy from the tears. Compassion floods his body and he nods with a smile. "Forgiven."

Julianne smiles big, presenting her white teeth, the two front ones slightly crooked from the rest. "Thank you. You're a sweetheart."

Pazmate grips her hand for the last time and releases it. As he flips his leg over the table bench, she adds sarcastically, "I knew underneath that uppity, snooty and arrogant, big-headed shield, there was a real down-to-earth person."

"Flattery will get you nowhere," he says, standing up. "Now do the dishes."

"Pazzz, can't you do it for me? That would be so sweet of you," she says flashing her long eyelashes, wet and black from running mascara.

"Wow, now that was pathetic," he says, laughing. "I don't think so. Later, alligator," he says, walking away from her, trying not to get his Dior shoes muddied from the recently watered grass.

"You're tough," she yells back at him, but he only waves his hand above his head without turning around. Looking back down at her worksheet, certain words smudged by tears she says, "After a while, crocodile."

FUTURE IS LOOKING BRIGHT

The guys realize that treatment is almost over and the real world awaits them. Yet there's a calmness in the air. They lie in the still blackness, a small light entering from a window, illuminating a stream of hope across the floor. Their bunk beds which used to symbolize a military hell, now whisper soft words that let them know everything is going to be okay.

"I can't believe it," Pete says staring at a stained ceiling panel. He finds a bird in the texture and an elephant as though the texturing were a cloudy summer's day. "In a few days, I will have completed this program. And I can't believe I'm going to say this, but—it's taught me a lot."

"I know what you mean," says another faceless voice. "It seems like we just got here yesterday. Time has really flown."

"Yeah, you've got that right," Charles says, joining the dark conversation. "It's funny, I really didn't expect to learn anything while being in treatment, but between my peers and counselors, I've learned more than I ever needed to."

All is silent for a moment when Pete adds, "I have learned things about myself that I never knew existed."

"I'm happy for you," Charles says, sarcastically. "Hey, what about you, Steve?" he asks, testing if he is still awake. "I bet you knew all this stuff already, being that you are an ex-caseworker and all." A few laughs crack into the dark.

"Yeah," Steve replies. "I knew the tools of recovery but it's only now that I'm finally learning how to apply the tools of recovery to my own life. I've gotten to see it from the other side of the desk."

"I feel you on that one," Marty says. "I am still finding it hard to believe how confident I've been feeling about myself lately."

"Me too," adds Charles. "Not that I wasn't already awesome. It's kind of strange. It's almost as if I had a spiritual awakening." All is quiet again and Marty starts picking at the loose thread he found in the mattress on his night of arrival. "Talking about spiritual awakenings," Charles continues, "before coming here and gaining insight about myself, I was convinced the way I was living was the only way of life for me."

"You're not alone," Steve replies. "It's amazing how clear things became for me once I removed the blinders and took the cotton out of my ears."

"Huh. Me too," Pete says. Not wanting to end the conversation, he asks, "Hey, Marty. What is the first thing you're going to do when you get out of treatment?"

"The first thing I'm going to do? Oh, man. When I get back home I'm going to get an In-and-Out burger . . . but then I'll call my sponsor and ask him to teach me how to work the twelve steps to recovery. What about you?"

"I'm going to go to a twelve-step meeting to get myself involved with a sponsor right away." Pete then addresses Charles with the same question, "What about you, Charles?"

"I'm going to call my ex-employer," he says sounding confident and determined. "See if I can get my old job back."

"You're thinking about going back to the oil fields?" Marty asks.

"Yeppers, little man," he says, convinced. "We've all gotta grow up sometime."

Marty is a little concerned. "Isn't that kind of risky—being that you're just getting out of treatment? I mean, you know the oil field has a reputation for substance abuse."

"Listen, my little friend, the way I figure it, substance abuse is everywhere, but I'm here to tell you that those safety guys are everywhere in the oil field screening for substance use. So it's not as bad as people think it is."

"He's right, Marty," Pete interjects. "Yes, our recovery should come first. However, we also have to earn a living."

"Yeah, I suppose you're right," Marty replies. "What about you, Steve? What are you going to do after treatment?"

"I think I'll go back to school."

"You have anything in mind?" Marty asks.

"I don't know. I'll figure it out. I just need to take it one day at a time."

"Hey, guys," says a pained Pazmate. "I'm really glad you all are excited about your recovery and your future plans, but you need to turn off the volume and go to sleep."

The hidden voices in the dark laugh, with a chorus of, "Sorry."

"Yeah, I gotta second that motion," Ben adds. "Chill out. Some of us are trying to sleep, you know."

"Whatever, Ben," a voice calls and the sound of a pillow hits Ben's bunk, but the darkness doesn't allow anyone to see if it is a clean shot.

There are a few moments of silence when Steve starts a *Walton's* goodnight sequence.

"Good night, Pete." A room of collective, hidden chuckles escapes into the room.

"Night, Steve. Goodnight, Marty."

"Good night, Steve. Goodnight, Charles."

"Good night, Steve. Night, Ben."

"Good night, Charles. Goodnight, Pazmate."

And somewhere in the darkness, the sound of Pazmate's sigh falls through the room.

IS THIS THE END?

Counselor Mike died the night before from his own hand. The next morning at the treatment center, Tim, the treatment center coordinator, breaks the news to his fellow counselors.

"**G**ood morning, Inky," Skeety says, playfully walking into the counselor's lounge.

"Good morning, Skeety," Inky replies, taking notice of Skeety's fancy appearance. "My, my, my," he says, "don't you look sharp as a tack today. What's the occasion?"

"Why thank you. I don't know what got into me," she says, pulling at the tuffs of her skirt. "I just felt the need to dress up this morning. Just enjoyin' bein' a one hundred percent woman, I guess."

"Well, I must admit, you're doing it and doing it well. You're looking quite dapper this morning. So anyway, back to business," Inky says, flirtatiously pushing Skeety away from the coffee maker. "What aftercare program are you setting your two graduating clients up with?"

"Mission Impossible Counseling. Afterall, they *do* deserve the best, Inky."

"Touché, Skeety. It doesn't get much better than M.I.C. Wow," Inky says bowing to Tim, the treatment center's administrator who has walked into the room. "This is a nice surprise. We usually don't have the pleasure of seeing the sensei out of his office until noon, how you been?"

"Don't mind Inky," Skeety says, knocking him out of the way. "I'm happy to see you anytime: morning, noon, or night."

But Tim is solemn as he takes his seat at the table. "Would you please close the treatment office door, Inky?"

The two counselors can see the stone look on Tim's face and are immediately concerned. Inky closes the door and they both sit across from Tim with their matching coffee mugs sitting on the table, their coffee gone placid from the chilled silence.

"You don't look so well," Skeety says, a lump growing in her throat. "What's wrong?"

"I have some bad news, counselors."

"What is it?" she asks looking at Inky to see if he's caught on.

But Inky doesn't know. "What is it, Tim?"

"Mike took his own life last night."

Skeety immediately tears up, covering her mouth with her hand.

Inky is reluctant to believe. "Hey man, don't play like . . . are you . . . it can't . . ." Inky's brain can't catch up to his mouth.

"I wish I wasn't serious."

Skeety's cries strengthen, so Inky wraps his right arm around her.

"Oh my . . . I just can't . . . I can't believe this."

"I know, Skeety. It's a hard thing to accept. I didn't want to believe it, either."

"How'd he do it?" Inky asks, his stare turned to stone. "How did he do such a thing?"

Tim takes a moment, adjusting in his seat and says, "My understanding is that he took a bottle of sleeping pills and never, and he never woke up again."

"No," Skeety whispers under her quivering lip. "This just can not be true," she says firmly, pressing her hands firmly on the table as though her adamancy might change something. "Why? Why, why, why would he do this?"

"I don't know," Tim answers, staring at the faux wood finish of the table. "No one knows why."

"Who found him?" Inky asks.

"I was told," Tim answers after swallowing the massive lump that is growing in his throat, "that his sister Lucero went over to his home this morning to have coffee and discovered him at the kitchen table."

"He just, he just didn't seem to be himself lately. He appeared so distant. Inky and I talked about that very thing two days ago over lunch. We should've . . ." and Skeety's voice trailed off.

"I guess sometimes, as professionals, we get so caught up in our client's needs that we forget to take care of ourselves," Inky adds, taping his coffee mug with his index finger.

"You're right about that. As professionals we also need to learn how to take care of ourselves," Skeety says, realizing that her hindsight is for nothing.

"Counselors, if any of you need counseling to work through this, I have arranged for a grief therapist to support you."

Tim, not knowing his place anymore, excuses himself from the table. Not looking at him as he leaves, they both say, "Thanks, Tim."

"You know what, Inky? I'm not sure, but . . ."

"What is it, Skeety?"

"Today is the day that treatment cries the blues."

EPILOGUE

A tall, slender woman with sandy blonde hair, pulled into a bun walks into a dimly lit room. Her eyes brilliant and wet behind thinly-framed glasses.

Mike's funeral was a week later. Even though the sky poured with sadness with days of crying and the confused looks on people's faces overwhelmed the burden of the earth, in a sort of strange kind of way, there was a calm, a cooling of hearts and spirits in the air. I couldn't help but think how peaceful Mike looked lying in that silver and bronze casket with the gold trimming his sisters picked out. Mike and I had worked together in this field called behavioral and mental health care for fifteen years. For those of you who have not experienced getting close to a co-worker, you may be missing out on a cherishable friendship. Mike was my friend . . . is my friend.

I spoke to Mike's sister, LaGail two days before the funeral, and by the time she finished telling me how much she and the rest of the family missed Mike, we were both lost in our tears. We couldn't distinguish whose salted stains belonged to whom. I couldn't help myself from wondering briefly how his children were doing. Yet, my judgment told me not to ask. So it was like LaGail read my mind when said the children were taking it hard, but one thing is for sure, Mike raised his children to be soldiers and by the Grace of God, they'll be okay. After reminiscing over Mike's memory, now speaking of him in the past tense,

LaGail and I gave each other a hug and went our separate ways, the common bond between us, broken.

I must confess that I was shocked when I saw Sharon at the cemetery standing next to the other farewell speakers, standing silent as though she felt that the others would judge her for being there. She stood so still as if hoping her body's silence would make her a forgotten shadow in the crowd. The first person to speak about Mike's memory as his body lay motionless in that custom-made casket was his sister, Debbie. After choking back tears and staring into the crowd of family members and friends for about two minutes, Debbie began to share her memories about how Mike started his late teenage years and early twenties on the wrong foot but through many hours of strong praying from their mother and the Grace of God, he was able to get himself back focus and change his life around. The calmness in the air reflected the same peace on Debbie's surrendered face, as she looked down at her brother lying in that casket before saying to him, as though we weren't there—"I love you." What else do you say? Debbie gave the microphone to her older brother, Raymond, and escorted herself to the front row of the family session and sat in her chair rocking as though she didn't have a worry in the world, a song sweeping the edge of her lips.

Raymond said, and I'll never forget it: "First, I would sadly like to share with you all that I wasn't around my little brother much because we lived in different states and over the years we rarely spoke to one another. Second, I would like to thank all of you for showing up for my brother's funeral. As I said, my brother and I didn't have much contact, but the one thing I admired most about my brother was that he was always inventing something to serve others. He truly cared about other people." And it wasn't so much what he said. Not the words he chose or the way he chose to say them, but that he came back to the fact that he didn't see Mike. They weren't close. They lived far away, and I knew: I knew what he was feeling. It was too late now. Raymond began to cry as he said, "Please, family and friends, don't judge harsh views about my brother." As the tears charged down Raymond's face in full force, he handed the microphone over to his sister Sonji LaFonda.

There was no doubt that Mike and Sonji LaFonda were siblings. These two were identical. The only difference was Sonji LaFonda's effeminate features.

She addressed the crowd. "Many of you, who know this family, know we lost our mother, father, and oldest sister, Alice in 1995." She paused. "And now here it is 2025 and we are laying our youngest brother to rest." She didn't look at us. Not us or the sky or at anything in particular outside of a patch of earth in front of her brother's grave. "Life is too short, unpredictable, and for those of you who have family and friends, today is the day to be part of their lives. Let them know how much they mean to you because . . ." She paused long enough for all of us to feel the Earth shift on its axis, but probably was only a few seconds. ". . . there is much truth in 'here today, gone tomorrow.'" Sonji LaFonda passed the microphone to her sister Lucero. Sonji LaFonda had recently retired from the U.S. Marine Corps after serving twenty-two years of full duty and her every move demonstrated that she was a steel Marine (Oorah) inside and out.

Lucero had always been the level-headed one and backbone of her siblings. She seemed to take ownership of that role as of 1995. Through a very brave and strong face, Lucero looked out into the crowd and spoke like an honest and integral leader: "There are many things that could be said about my brother. But the one thing I would like to say and will forever cherish about Mike is that he was a good brother and I knew that if I ever needed my brother, he would be there. Thank you." With a firm grip, the microphone hung by her side. It is what happened next that surprised me. As Lucero turned to stand by her family, Sharon, the shadow in a black, knee-length dress and string of chipped pearls hanging from around her neck held out her delicate hand, reaching for the microphone asking, "Please, may I?" Lucero looked momentarily at her family looking for approval and handed the microphone to the small-framed, white woman.

"You don't know me," she said, looking at Mike's friends and family. "I'm Sharon and I was one of Mike's clients." Her lip began to quiver, hiding itself within her mouth. "But I am not what you would call a typical client. I hated Mike," she said, hating herself for its truth. "And for no reason other than he was black." I looked at his family, waiting for a response, an outburst, but it didn't come. Their stances in the wet soil changed, their heads tilted to the other direction, but no words came from their mouths. "Call it the Grace of God or—a miracle, but Mike didn't give up on me. I'm sure I'll never know why," she laughed under her tears. "I discovered something. I discovered how to live and I learned how to live clean and sober and to judge people by their character and not by the color of their skin. To be honest with you all, I've never really had anyone. At least, no one I would consider a positive influence, but Counselor Mike showed me to look at the world a little differently. I would like to give his family my condolences. Mike wasn't my brother. I don't know how he got that scar over his left eyebrow or how he took his coffee. I don't know what made him laugh or how y'all spent Christmas. I just know he taught *me* how to laugh. Seems so simple, but . . ." She looked down at Mike's casket and said, "I hope, 'thank you' is enough."

We all walked away from the gravesite that day like defeated children who have suffered disappointment. But Sharon stood there. She stood silent as Mike's family sat down into the black limousine that would take them back to Sonji LaFonda's house for a potluck. She stood there as I shook my umbrella and placed it in the backseat of my blue bronco and she stood there as the cemetery employees stood close by like vultures waiting for larger animals to leave the prey, waiting hesitantly so they could cover my friend in soil.

As I said earlier, Mike and I went way back. He was my friend . . . is my friend. I'm going to miss him and so will many others.

Bye, Mike

Dedicated to:

The loving memory of Michael Lendell Jones

April 11, 1967 – September 13, 2025

TREATMENT CRIES THE BLUES: A CRY FOR HELP

Suicide in the United States
- Suicide is a common and increasing tragedy that affects many lives.
- Hundreds of thousands of people attempt or commit suicide every year.
- Elderly people are the most common age group to attempt or commit suicide.
- Suicide is the third leading cause of death for people between the ages of 15–24.
- If the person gets the proper help, suicide is usually preventable.
- By understanding the warning signs, you may someday help someone from committing suicide.
- There are many reasons a person thinks of committing suicide:
  - Sometimes a person may feel very depressed and think suicide is their only escape.
  - Mental illness and personality disorders are also reasons that a person may attempt or commit suicide.
  - Alcohol and drug use also can be a factor. While under the influence, the reasoning ability is reduced which can lead to an accidental or irrational decision to attempt or commit suicide.
  - Sometimes family history plays a role. A person who has lost a loved one through suicide may also choose to attempt or commit suicide.
  - People who have a low level of the brain chemical, serotonin, may be at a higher risk of suicide.

- Sometimes people with chronic illnesses attempt or commit suicide. They may feel that ending their lives is better than suffering with their illness.
- Women are more likely to *attempt* suicide during a crisis. Men, however, are more likely to *succeed* in committing suicide during a crisis.
- Native Americans and Anglos have higher suicide rates than other groups.
- Married people have a lower suicide rate than those who are single, widowed, or divorced.
- Suicide is more common among people who are unemployed.

Some Common Myths about Suicide

Myth: Talking about suicide may give a person the idea.

Fact: People who are suicidal already have the idea. Discussing suicide can help prevent a person from acting on it.

Myth: People who make unsuccessful suicide attempts are only trying to seek attention.

Fact: Often, a suicide attempt is a way to get attention—it's the person reaching out for help. Dismissing the incident only makes the matter worse. If the person doesn't get proper help, he or she may make a more serious suicide attempt next time.

Myth: Once people are suicidal, they can no longer be helped.

Fact: The crisis period sometimes lasts only for a limited time. However, a person can get help and improve. Remember, another crisis can occur. It's important to take each occurrence seriously and get the person the help they need.

Warning Signs:
- People may threaten to take their lives. They may say, "It's no use to live," or "Nothing really matters."
- They may make unexpected changes in their lives, or start giving their personal possessions away.
- They may start withdrawing from family and friends and often appear depressed.
- They may have a change in mood like going from sad to happy. Such a sudden mood change could mean they are relieved because their problems will soon end.
- They may experience changes in sexual, sleeping, or eating habits.
- People who have attempted suicide before may attempt suicide again.

Emotional Support:
- Show a person who is suicidal that you care by taking their feelings seriously.
- Listen to them and help them discuss their feelings. Explain to them that they can recover and professional help is available.
- Don't argue, challenge, reason, or try to analyze the suicidal person's motives.
- Help the person view their reasons to live and help them see that no problem is too big to solve.

When suspecting that someone is about to make a suicide attempt:
- Immediately get help. In an emergency, call 911. Do not leave the person alone until help arrives.
- Try to keep the person from using drugs and alcohol. Alcohol and drug use can impair a person's thinking.
- Become aware of your local suicide hotline, and become a volunteer at a crisis prevention center that will help those in need.

Remember: The more you know about suicide and the warning signs, the greater chance you have of helping someone in need.

Become aware of how you can help.

TREATMENT CRIES THE BLUES

THE MUSICAL

TREATMENT CRIES THE BLUES

Synopsis of Scenes

The Time: Early 21ˢᵗ Century
The Place: Farmington, New Mexico

Act I

Introduction

	Scene 1	This is a White World—Mike's Office
	Scene 2	I know! You Rich! Bipolar person!—Clients' Lounge
	Scene 3	What's the Problem?—Therapy Group
Stage time	Scene 4	Antisocialist Manipulation Plot—Dining Room
31 minutes	Scene 5	Gangster Love—Outside Bench Area
	Scene 6	Who's Angry?—Assignment Group

Act II

	Scene 1	Gaining Courage to Set Boundaries—Clients' Lounge
	Scene 2	Hotline, Hotline, Calling on the Hotline—Mike's Office
Stage time	Scene 3	Too Many People have Problems—Mike's Office
30 minutes	Scene 4	Supporting Hurt Feelings—Dining Room
	Scene 5	Don't Quit before the Miracle Happens—Outside Bench Area
	Scene 6	Read My Lips, Spiritual Awakening—Dining Room

Act III

	Scene 1	I Can See Clearly Now the Rain is Gone—Counselor's Office
	Scene 2	Clients' Discussion—Group Room
	Scene 3	Building Self-esteem—Group Room
Stage time	Scene 4	We're Precious Souls—Clients' Lounge
34 minutes	Scene 5	It's Time to Get Honest—Outside Bench Area
	Scene 6	What is the Good Stuff?—Group Room

Act IV

	Scene 1	He Doesn't Seem Right—Counselor's Office
	Scene 2	Hope for a Better Day—Mike's Office
	Scene 3	Family Reunion—Outside Bench Area
Stage time	Scene 4	It's Called Bipolar—Outside
29 minutes	Scene 5	The Future is Looking Bright—Clients' Bedroom
	Scene 6	Is this the End?—Counselor's Office

Treatment Cries the Blues

Song Selection

(Lead vocals Terry, backup sound choir). Act I, Scene 3

(Lead vocals Minnie, backup sound choir). Act I, Scene 5

(Lead vocals Julianne, backup sound choir). Act II, Scene 1

(Lead vocals Mike, backup sound choir). Act II, Scene 2

(Lead vocals Ben, backup sound choir). Act II, Scene 5

(Lead vocals Pazmate, backup sound choir). Act II, Scene 6

(Lead vocals Sharon, backup sound choir). Act III, Scene 4

(Lead vocals Skeety and Inky, backup sound choir). Act IV, Scene 1

(Vocals Charles, Marty, Pete, and Steve, backup sound choir). Act IV, Scene 5

(Vocals Administrator, Skeety, and Inky, backup sound choir). Act IV, Scene 6

Treatment Cries the Blues

Performing Cast

Administrator Tim (White male "song")

Ben (Indian male "song")

Charles (Hispanic male "song")

Skeety (Hispanic female "song")

Inky (White male "song")

Skeety (Hispanic female "song")

Inky (White male "song")

Julianne (White female "song")

Marty (Indian male "song")

Mike (Black male "song")

Minnie (Black female "song")

Pazmate (White male "song")

Pete (White male "song")

Sharon (White female "song")

Steve (White male "song")

Terry (White female "song")

INTRODUCTION

(Courtroom Scene) Adlibbing

FUTURE CLIENTS
(Adlibbing) (They're talking amongst themselves.)

BAILIFF
All rise.

FUTURE CLIENTS
(Everyone rises.)

JUDGE COX
(Enters the courtroom)
You may all be seated.

FUTURE CLIENTS
(Everyone sits down.)

JUDGE COX
After carefully reviewing each of your probation officer's progress reports, I have noticed each of you has been found guilty of an alcohol or drug-related charge. Therefore, within the powers granted to me by the people of the state of New Mexico, I sentence each of you to ninety days of residential treatment at the Mission Impossible Counseling program.

FUTURE CLIENTS
(Moans and groans)

JUDGE COX

By chance any of you don't complete the Mission Impossible Counseling program within the next six months, you will be found in contempt of court and a bench warrant will be issued for your arrest. The remainder of your one-year probation will be served at the county detention center.

FUTURE CLIENTS
(Continue to moan and groan)

JUDGE COX

Probation Officer, do you have anything to add to the court's conditions?

PROBATION OFFICER

No, your honor. I think everyone can benefit from residential treatment if the opportunity is appropriately utilized. I understand that the Mission Impossible Counseling program is an outstanding one.

JUDGE COX

Bailiff!

BAILIFF

Yes, your honor?

JUDGE COX

Please assist these ladies and gentlemen out of my courtroom.

BAILIFF

Alright, ladies and gentlemen, let's go.

(The bailiff, probation officer, and all the future clients exit the courtroom.)

JUDGE COX

(The judge asks the audience to bow their heads as he says a prayer for all the suffering alcoholics, drug addicts, and families who suffer as a result.)

ACT I: THIS IS A WHITE WORLD

(Scene 1: Mike's Office)

MIKE
(Speaking in a warm and welcoming tone)
Hello, how are you doing? My name is Mike and I will be your primary counselor while you're in treatment. If you have any questions about what will be expected from you while you're in treatment, this is your time to discuss any concerns or needs.

SHARON
(Speaking in a low, but sarcastic tone)
I've a question. Do you really think I'm going to open up and tell you anything about my personal life? Because frankly counselor sir, my life is none of your damn business. However, my brilliant, self-titled probation officer came up with the genius of an idea that I need treatment, so here I am. Hi!

MIKE
You know, it seems to me you're not happy to be here.

SHARON
Hey, yer quick! It didn't take you long to figure that one out.

MIKE
No, it didn't, and now that we both can agree you are angry, what would you like to do about it? How willing are you to address the core of your anger?

SHARON
(Challenging Mike's authority)
You really want to know why I'm angry and what makes me angry?

MIKE

Yes, I would indeed.

SHARON

(Speaking slowly and coldly. Enunciating each syllable)
Niggers. Niggers just like you.

MIKE

(Keeping his calm)
So, I'm beginning to understand that I make you angry. However, I do not understand what behavior or action I am doing to trigger your anger.

SHARON

I don't like you and just me being in the same room with you is upsettin'. Is that too hard for you to get?

MIKE

Well, the good news is you don't have to like me nor do I have to like you. One thing is for sure though, you are in treatment and while you are here we both need to put our heads together and figure out the best plan so you will never have to come back to see me or anyone like me again.

SHARON

(Her tone and body language demonstrate her disbelief.)
Again? In case you'd missed it, I don't want to be here now!

MIKE

(Speaking in a firm yet compassionate tone)
Sharon, I would like to inform you that we do not have locked doors here. Anytime you feel you would like to leave treatment, that is your choice. I also would like to inform you that if you want to stay in treatment and work on the issues that led to the behaviors that brought you here, that would be another choice. Life is all about making choices.

SHARON
(Says defiantly)
Yeah, some choice. 'Cause if I did decide to walk out of these "so-called" unlocked doors, the genius you think yourself to be would likely make a call to my probation officer and I'd be back in jail.

MIKE
Now that you are realizing the power of choice, what choices are you willing to make for yourself? While you're pondering on that, I need you to complete this "feeling journal" and return it back to me two days from now. That is of course if you choose to stay in treatment.

(He gives Sharon her feeling journal and she exits his office.)

I know! You Rich! Bipolar person!

(Scene 2: Clients' Lounge)

(Scene takes place in the lounge where clients gather between groups. Pazmate and Steve are throwing sarcastic remarks at each other while Julianne referees.)

PAZMATE

Hey, Steve, I notice you were giving Charles advice earlier during the meditation group, but I can't help but wonder that if you are such a great counselor, I mean, *ex-case worker* with such great advice, why are you, with all your greatness, in treatment?

JULIANNE
(She says to Pazmate)

Why don't you just back off? At least Steve tries being supportive. You, on the other hand, have not shared one thing about yourself, except that you are wealthy and come from a wealthy family.

PAZMATE

And? I'm sorry. Would you all like it if I told you I was a poor underachiever with parents who could not pay the mortgage and a family friend or a loved one abused me as a child? Oh, sh—I almost forgot, so please keep this our little secret, uh, I kicked the family dog when I was a kid.

JULIANNE

No, but I don't think it would hurt if you decided to get real and accept the fact that even though you are wealthy, your substance abuse has caused problems for you and others.

STEVE
(To Julianne)

Don't even worry about it. I have seen people of his kind fail at treatment time and time again.

(Addressing Pazmate)
And would you like to know the reason why?

PAZMATE
(Sarcastically uninterested)
Not really.

STEVE
(In a sarcastically pedantic voice)
Well, today is your lucky day, because I'm going to tell you anyway. You see, it goes like this Paz: there are "certain" groups of people who are under the illusion that they can control their outcome when they are under the influence of alcohol or drugs. They just can't seem to understand why other people make such a big deal about their usage. You see, Pazmate, with that way of thinking, they block the avenue which allows valuable information to enter the brain that is highly needed to comprehend a simple formula that will allow them to live one day at a time clean and sober.

PAZMATE
(Acting impressed)
Wow. So tell me junior counselor Steve, how long does it take a counselor like you to comprehend the simple formula?

JULIANNE
(Annoyed)
Why don't both of you just give it a rest?

PAZMATE
Sure, Mommy dearest. As much as I hate to miss the rest of the two's lame-brains conversation, I believe I'd be more entertained by reading my new subscription of Money Week and bore myself with details of how people of *class* live such as me.

(Pazmate leaves with a smirk on his face.)

STEVE
(Addressing Julianne)

He just doesn't get it, does he?

JULIANNE
(Shakes her head)

Although, I do have to say, Pazmate is right about one thing.

STEVE

Oh, yeah? What's that?

JULIANNE

Don't think I'm trying to clown on you, but you do come on as though you have the answers for everyone else's problems. I have to be honest with you, I hardly hear you speak about your own issues. Pazmate is kinda right. You are very supportive toward the rest of us and I do realize you've been a caseworker for many years, yet the formula you talk about—does it apply to you?

STEVE
(Defensively)

I don't have to listen to this. I'm not even going to entertain your comment. I still have my autobiography to write, my counselor's been bugging me to get it done. I guess I'll talk with you later.

(Steve leaves in a state of confusion as to why Julianne is attacking him. Moments later, Julianne sighs and then leaves in the opposite direction.)

What's the Problem?

(Scene 3: Therapy Group)

(Scene takes place in the therapy room. Terry is irritated and does not want to hear anything anyone has to say about her problematic drinking habit.)

PETE

Terry, what about you? You've been here going on two weeks and you still seem to carry a resentment toward the judge who referred you to treatment.

TERRY
(Snapping at Pete)

I don't know what you're talking about.

MIKE
(Speaking to Terry)

Come on. I think you know very well what he is talking about.

TERRY
(Speaking angrily)

Okay, you want me to say it? Yes, I'm very resentful about being in treatment. How would you feel if you were treated like a common criminal?

MIKE
(Addressing Terry)

Would you mind elaborating for us what you mean by that?

TERRY
(Speaking in a calm yet irritable tone)

Look, I'll be the first to admit that I like to have a drink every now and then. But that judge had no right to send me here because I *am not* an alcoholic nor do I have a drinking problem.

MARTY
(Challenging Terry)

Hey, I've heard you say on many occasions that you don't have a drinking problem. I've also heard you share about the fifteen DWIs you've received.

TERRY
(In defense)

That's my point exactly. Just because I have a couple of margaritas, our so-called law enforcers have the audacity to promote the badge that reads "to protect and serve" citizens of this country, when they really have nothing better to do than to harass law-abiding people like me.

MINNIE
(Accusatory tone)

Yo, Terry! Instead of complaining and blaming the legal system for your crap, maybe you should start taking responsibility for your drinking.

TERRY
(Belittling Minnie)

Again—my point exactly. Instead of wasting taxpayer's money by hauling me off to jail because I had a little drink, our police committee should spend more time and resources apprehending gangbangers and common thugs.

MIKE

Terry, need I remind you that we are here to support one another's recovery, not to attack our peers when they give us feedback that we don't like or agree with.

BEN
(With sincerity)

Besides, you may not realize this but you are fortunate to even be in treatment.

TERRY
(Sarcastically)

Yippee! Fortunate me.

BEN
(Speaking with emotion)

You know, the unfortunate ones never make it to treatment. They end up in wheelchairs or worse—cemeteries. Or take a good friend of mine: he chose to drink and drive which ended by him killing two family members and is now serving twenty-four years in a state penitentiary.

MIKE

Okay, it seems like we're out of time, so if no one has anything else they would like to add, let's close this group with "Hope for a Better Day."

(The group forms a circle and holds hands.)

Hope for a better day, hope I will laugh and play, hope I will find the way, hope for a better day.

(After the group leaves, Terry stays back in the group room continuing to fill the "victim role." She sings [Song Selection].)

Antisocialist Manipulation Plot

(Scene 4: Dining Room)

(Charles' antisocial manipulating behaviors appear as Marty begins to set boundaries.)

CHARLES
(Being charismatic)

Hey, Marty. I don't know what it was, but something I must have eaten during lunch really has my stomach upset. Normally it's not my style to ask favors from anyone, however, today is a special occasion. So whatcha say, bro? How about sweeping and mopping the dining area for me?

MARTY
(Nervously)

Listen, man, I don't want you to be mad at me, but my counselor and I have been working on me becoming more assertive and setting boundaries for myself. One way for me to start setting boundaries is to stop letting other people talk me into doing their chores.

CHARLES
(Pushing the issue)

Come on, bro. You can't allow these counselors to run your life. If you do, they'll brainwash you. Listen to me, you have to stay strong, little man. If there is one thing I learned while in the joint and hopefully you'll learn this someday as well, it's us against them.

MARTY
(Standing more firmly)

I'm sorry, Charles. Maybe I don't understand the prison mentality and hopefully I'll never go there to learn it, but if there is one thing I do know it's that I'm tired of the way I've been living. So if that means it takes brainwashing for me to live a happy, joyous life, well, I hope these counselors brainwash the hell out of me.

CHARLES
(Intimidating)
Little man, you are so weak. I've seen guys like you fall many times in the joint. I'll bet you couldn't last one week where I've been.

MARTY
(Sees Charles for what he's doing and becomes more assertive)
Maybe you're right, but if you stop being your own worst enemy, not even you would have to go back to the horrible places you have been.

CHARLES
Whatever. You just don't get it, do you, little man? How can you be so blind that you can't see that all of this is a government conspiracy?

MARTY
(Realizes he's stronger than Charles)
Government conspiracy? Okay, if you say so. Anyhow, I still have my relapse prevention packet that I need to complete. I better get started on it before my counselor comes down on me hard. I hope you start to feel better, Charles. I'll talk to you later.

CHARLES
(Speaking rudely)
You really think you have this thing all figured out don't you, little man? Little do you know, unknown to your knowledge, you will soon see they're out to get you as well as me. Move it, you're blocking my way. I need to finish sweeping the floor.
(Attempting to push past Marty)

MARTY
(Marty stands firm)
"Excuse me" would be nice, don't you think?

CHARLES
(Defeated)
There's no excuse for you. You seem to have been born that way.

MARTY
Charles? What are the magic words?

CHARLES
Excuse me! Little man.

(Charles says as he walks past Marty.)

Gangster Love

(Scene 5: Outside Bench Area)

(Scene takes place outside on the clients' bench table. Ben does not want to discuss his relationship with his father and cannot believe how Minnie tries to justify her gang life.)

BEN
(Speech and manner suggest defense)
I don't want to talk about it anymore!

MINNIE
(Pushing the issue)
Why do you feel like it's your fault that your father has lung cancer?

BEN
(Toying, but serious)
Look, girl, you've been my friend since the day we entered treatment together. I really do respect your "little miss gangster" booty for accepting me for who I am. You go friend girl! But please lose something, honey. Keep your pretty little nose out of my business when it comes to my family affairs.

MINNIE
(She becomes angry and then is able to calm herself.)
Oh, no you didn't! Don't you be tryin' to come at me with attitude. I hear you, though. I'll back off.

BEN
(Speaking in a feminine tone)
Thanks, Minnie. You're such a dear friend.

MINNIE
(Changing subject)
So where will you live when you leave treatment?

BEN
(Confused and sad)
To be honest with you Minnie—I'm clueless.

MINNIE
(Said coyly)
You know, I would invite you to come and kick it with me Ben . . .

BEN
(Laughing)
On Elm Street, in the hood?

MINNIE
(Jokingly)
Like I was saying, Money, I would but I kinda like you and I kinda would like to see you stay alive.

BEN
(In his gangster impression)
You jive pigeon! Could you imagine me riding with the Dirty Crips 20s?

MINNIE
(Trying to picture it)
Honestly, I can't even fathom the thought.

BEN
What? You don't think I can fight? Girl, I can sock someone in their nose and make it bleed and kick someone in their stomach.

(Ben demonstrates how tough he is by air fighting.)

MINNIE
(Serious)
See, Ben, that is what most people think. They believe all we do in the hood is go roun' beatin' people up, robbing and sellin' drugs.

BEN
(Hesitant)

Hello. Earth to Minnie. Unless I misunderstood something, you are a gang member, are you not? So if you are . . . *Minnie put your fists in your pockets . . .* Please correct me if I'm wrong, don't gangsters—whup booty?

MINNIE
(Irritated)

Do you think I joined the Dirty Crips 20s just because I want to go and beat someone up?

BEN
(Sincere)

Well, then why did you become a gang member?

MINNIE
(Assertive)

The same reason people join the U.S. Army: to help defend and protect the hood and the people who live there.

BEN
(Disbelief)

Wow. Oh, Minnie. That is so much bull. You cannot convince me that illegal activities in your neighborhood are patriotic events.

MINNIE
(Trying to gain empathy)

Look, man, my mother struggled to work two and three dead-end jobs at a time, just to keep us all fed. She never brought harm to anyone her entire adult life. But you know what, Benny? We were always hungry and cold during the wintertime. Then, when I was twelve, I joined the Dirty Crips 20s. You can bet my family ain't hungry anymore.

BEN
(Still argumentative)
So, friend girl, in your mind that makes you a patriot?

MINNIE
(Serious)
Yes, sir. And it makes me and mine fed. You may not understand it, but like the U.S. Army, we defend and protect ours.

BEN
(Feeling defeated)
Okay.

(Ben sighs)
It's your story, tell it how you like. Anyway, sorry to jump off ship, but I gotta bounce. I still have my self-esteem packet to work on. Catch you later, Minnie.

(Ben leaves Minnie standing there.)

MINNIE
Okay, see ya.

(Minnie's soldier mentality kicks in and she sings [Song Selection].)

Who's Angry?

(Scene 6: Assignment Group)

(Pete and Minnie are expressing their views.)

MINNIE
(Minnie has just shared a personal experience with the group.)
Yo, and that's the way it is, dogg!

PETE
(Frustrated over Minnie's attitude)
To whom are you calling a dog? Do you see any dogs in here?

MINNIE
(Confrontational)
Homie, you need to just chill out, you heard?

PETE
(Sarcastic to express his dislike towards Minnie's attitude)
Did I hear what? I'm standing right here, of course, I heard you, though I have to say that *you* haven't really said anything except jibber jabber.

MIKE
(Trying to defuse the situation)
Both of you need to calm down.

PETE
(Irritated)
I am tired of the gangbanger running off at the mouth.

MINNIE
(Exuding strength)
So what are you gonna do about it?

PETE
(More frustrated)
It's big mouths like you that make men like me, abuse women.

MINNIE
(With her battle face on)
Wrong! You become abusive towards women because you're too afraid to confront a man.

PETE
(Angry)
You stupid, little—

MIKE
(Authoritative tone)
That's enough from both of you.

SHARON
(Hesitant, but feeling cocky enough to voice her opinion)
Pete is right though. Some of us don't understand nor do we want to understand "homeboy" and "homegirl" talk.

JULIANNE
(To Sharon)
Still, I don't think any man has the right to put his hands on a woman in an abusive way.

MIKE
(Trying to clarify the truth about violent acts)
I agree with that, however, the truth is, no one should be abusive toward another human under any circumstance.

STEVE
(With a look of a sudden epiphany)
That is so true. In *my* field of work, I have seen abuse on both sides of genders and the results are always the same: someone ends up being hurt or disappointed.

MIKE
(Calming the group)
Alright now, this group is coming to a close. After group, I need Minnie and Pete to go talk with their primary counselors about what happened in group today.

(All groups close with clients forming a circle holding hands and saying "Hope for a Better Day" chant.)

ACT II: GAINING COURAGE TO SET BOUNDARIES

(Scene 1: Clients' Lounge Area)

JULIANNE
(Hysterical)

I can't believe that she wants me to stop spending time with my male peers. This is treatment? I thought this is where we came to practice our social skills!

MINNIE
(Used to Julianne's drama, but sick of it)

Did your counselor request for you to stop socializing with the male clients *completely*? Or did she ask you not to socialize with them *so much*?

JULIANNE
(Defensive)

Does it really matter how much I talk with the men? It's not as if I'm sleeping with any of them.

MINNIE
(Confrontational)

Julianne, I really hate to shake you off your throne, but as I see it, you *do* spend most of your time hanging out with the men.

JULIANNE
(Defensive and projecting)

Oh really, Minnie? Does it bother you?

MINNIE
(Scoffs)

Why should it? However, where I come from we keep it real with each other, and I'm just trying to kick a little flavor to you.

JULIANNE
(Playing the victim)
Hey, I know you don't mean any harm, but the truth of the matter is I feel more comfortable being around males than females. I just seem to trust men more. Women are always out to get one another.

MINNIE
(Not dropping the issue)
I think you are confusing trust with manipulation. Like I said, I ain't tryin' to con you. I must stay real with you.

JULIANNE
(Confused)
What do you mean?

MINNIE
(Jokingly, but seriously)
Come on, Julianne, I've seen you. I've seen you bat those big soft eyes and speak in that sweet innocent voice, stickin' your business in men's faces and I've watched them trip over their own feet to serve you.

JULIANNE
(Defensive)
That is not true, Minnie!

MINNIE
Oh, so now you're trying to con me?

JULIANNE
(Projecting)
No! And even if it were true, my counselor has no right to insinuate that I am male-dependent.

MINNIE
(With an encouraging, supportive tone)
Julianne, has it occurred to you that maybe your counselor isn't out to get you? That maybe she actually cares about your well-being and wants

to help you get your children out of foster care because right now you are struggling with caring for yourself?

JULIANNE
(Feels a little stunned and emotional to the new realization)
I love my children very much. I just feel so ashamed about what I've put them through. I don't deserve their love. I don't think I can ever forgive or love myself again.

MINNIE
(Showing compassion for her friend)
Yes, you can. Just take it one step and one day at a time.

(Enter Charles)

CHARLES
Hey, Julianne, how about helping me with my relapse prevention packet?

JULIANNE
(Finally establishing boundaries)
I think your primary counselor is more qualified to help you than I am.

CHARLES
(Confused by Julianne's new confidence)
Man, what's gotten into you?

(Taking exit)

JULIANNE
(Smiling)
Bye, Charles.

MINNIE
(Enjoying Julianne's victory)
My girl!

(They give each other a hug and Minnie exits. Julianne sings [Song Selection].)

Hotline, Hotline, Calling on the Hotline

(Scene 2: Mike's Office)

(Mike's phone conversation with his ex-spouse in his office)

MIKE
(Trying to stay calm)
Hello. This is not the time to talk about this.

(Getting agitated)
What do you want from me?

(Frustration building)
I cannot afford to pay more child support.

No! You will not keep me out of my children's life.

(Attempting to calm himself)
Why can't you just get on with your life and let me live mine?

Another thing, when you need to talk with me in a non-emergency situation concerning our children, would you please call me at home and not at my job?

(Anger returns)
Why? ... Why? Why do you continue to blame me for your unhappiness? You were the one who walked out of the marriage.

(Trying to be reasonable)
Do you have any idea what you are putting our children through? Our children are scared to death of that man you have them living with!

(Not letting it go)
This is not about you or me. This is about me trying to protect our children from a possible lifetime of unresolved hurt.

What?

Are you serious?

(Flabbergasted)
You're sincerely trying to convince yourself that I'm upset because you are with him?

(With sincerity)
On the contrary, I am happy the two of you are together.

(Realization of his children's safety upsets him.)
However, I'm very afraid when I think of the dangers you are setting our children up for.

I wouldn't have dreamt in a million years that someday I would be in a battle with my ex-wife fighting to keep our children out of harm's way.

You know what? Do what you feel you must do, but remember our children are the ones who will ultimately pay the price! Bye!

(Mike slams the phone down and storms out of his office.)

(Mike comes back into his office moments later. He appears a bit calmer and he sings [Song Selection].)

Too Many People Have Problems

(Scene 3: Mike's Office)

MIKE
(Friendly and accommodating)
Sharon, come on in and take a seat. Would you like to tell me what's going on?

SHARON
(Agitated and playing stupid)
Tell you what?

MIKE
(Making it clear that he's in no mood)
We are not going to play this little game today. You know exactly what I'm talking about.

SHARON
(Testing Mike's patience)
You talkin' 'bout my conversation with Ben?

MIKE
(Firmly)
That's it. Would you like to tell me why you felt the need to attack Ben?

SHARON
(Sarcastic)
I didn't. I called him a faggot. He is gay.

MIKE
(Not in any mood to deal with Sharon's sarcasm)
Sharon, that kind of language is not acceptable here, so to ensure you from using such words again while you're in treatment, I'm putting you on a behavioral contract.

SHARON
(Projecting)
This place is so screwed up. Counselors tell us to be honest with our peers and to give each other feedback but when we do, we get put on a behavioral contract.

MIKE
(Not letting her project)
First off, let's not talk about "we" behaviors. Let's stay focused on *your* behaviors. So tell me, what's to be accomplished by calling Ben a derogatory name?

SHARON
(Defending her stance)
He's gay! You don't have a problem with that?

MIKE
(Still not allowing her to displace her issues)
We're not here to discuss what I have a problem with. However, we can discuss how Ben being gay affects your recovery.

SHARON
(Still projecting out and thinking herself clever)
It's just not right! It's supposed to be Adam and Eve, not Adam and Steve.

MIKE
(Pushing Sharon into self-examination)
So here is what I understand, you disagree with the way some people choose to live their lives. That's fair and it's your right. However, what I'm asking you is: how do other people's lifestyles affect you?

SHARON
(Remains sarcastic)
Well, I guess if the whole world became like Ben, that'd be one way to cure the world of the population problem.

MIKE
(Confrontational)

I've heard you speak of having problems with people who are of a different ethnic race than you. I've heard you speak of having a problem with Ben's sexuality, and I have even heard you speak of having a problem with the legal system . . .

SHARON
(Continues being sarcastic)

Did you have a point?

MIKE
(Put out, but not beaten)

My point *is:* I have not heard you speak much about Sharon and her problems. Obviously your probation officer did not recommend you to treatment because everything in your life is wonderful.

SHARON
(Defending herself)

There really isn't much to tell, Mike!

MIKE
(Hitting her with the truth)

You know, you are *right* where you are supposed to be.

SHARON
(Confused and angry)

Oh, really? How did you come to that conclusion, Mr. Counselor?

MIKE

Let me simplify it for you. Most people do not come into treatment doing backflips and cartwheels because they are so happy to be here. But now that you *are* here, it's up to you to decide what you want out of your time.

SHARON
(Showing mild concern)

Does my probation officer have to know about me being put on a behavioral contract?

MIKE

Yes. I send out weekly progress reports. But try to remember, a behavioral contract is your agreement to discontinue the behavior of what you are doing.

SHARON
(Returning to her former, defensive demeanor)

Whatever. My probation officer is a jerk.

MIKE

I see you've found another person with a problem.

SHARON
(Angry)

They're not exactly hard to find!

MIKE
(Taking the little victory he has made)

Anyhow, if you just sign right here, we'll bring this session to an end.

SHARON

Good, I'm really getting sleepy. These sessions are so boring.

(Sharon signs the behavioral contract and walks out of Mike's office without saying another word.)

Supporting Hurt Feelings

(Scene 4: Dining Area)

TERRY
(Starting to feel good about herself)
I really have been thinking about what my peers and counselors have been saying. I am finally beginning to see that just because I haven't hurt anyone else or myself physically, that does not excuse my reckless drinking behaviors.

PETE
(Empathizing)
It's hazy to me, because I also think this place is helping me understand my emotions better. I'm really glad my primary counselor helps me to understand the importance of making amends to Minnie. She and I get along so much better now.

TERRY
I don't mean to get too personal. I realize I'm not your primary counselor . . . it's just that I am interested about how it felt when you became abusive toward your partners.

PETE
(Embarrassed with his past behavior)
Shame. A lot of shame. But now that I'm in treatment, I've learned that I used to mask my shame with anger.

TERRY
(Curious)
Have you discovered what triggers the shame?

PETE
(Shame fading)
My counselor and I have been working on that. I am led to believe that my own insecurities of not being good enough, and trying to be a perfectionist are at the root of it.

TERRY

What would happen when things didn't go the way you thought they should or how you wanted them to go?

PETE

I exploded. And I'd usually look for the weakest target.

TERRY

Who might that be?

PETE

(Becoming angry)

Anyone who cared about me: parents, children, spouses, close friends . . . you name it.

TERRY

(Recognizing Pete's discomfort)

Why did you rage at the people who care about you?

PETE

(Flooding with emotion)

I don't know. My insecurities made me feel safe, I guess. I figured if they cared about me, they wouldn't hurt me.

TERRY

(Trying to understand)

So . . . it became a vicious cycle? Shame turns to anger and so on.

PETE

(Feeling hopeful)

Yeah, and now that I understand more about my feelings, I have begun working on my insecurities.

TERRY
(Happy for Pete and herself)
You know as well as I do that I hated the judge who sent me here, but now I think that coming to treatment is the best thing that happened to me since . . . I don't know when.

PETE
Tell me about it.

(Pete and Terry give each other a hug and then go to the next group.)

Don't Quit Before the Miracle Happens

(Scene 5: Outside Bench Area)

BEN
(Jittery)

I am so scared.

CHARLES

About what?

BEN
(With nervous excitement)

Haven't you heard? My parents are coming to see me tomorrow!

CHARLES
(Happy for Ben)

Your mom and dad?

BEN

Yes, yes, both of them!

CHARLES
(Confused)

Well, why are you scared? I thought you *wanted* your parents to come support you during family day.

BEN
(Anxious)

I do, I do, but—to be honest with you, my father disowned me ten years ago when he found out I was gay.

CHARLES
(Concerned)

So why do you think he's coming to see you now?

BEN
(Lost in thought)
I'm not sure. I did find out about two months ago that my father has been diagnosed with lung cancer.

(Enter Marty)

MARTY
(In a good mood)
Hey, what are you two being so secretive about?

CHARLES
(Serious)
Ben was just telling me that his parents are coming to see him tomorrow for family day.

MARTY
(Somewhat unaware)
That's good news.

BEN
(Confused)
I just don't know how I should feel.

CHARLES
(Jokingly)
Have you tried with your hands?

BEN
(Trying to humor Charles' humor)
Wow, stop making funnies. You know what I mean.

MARTY
(Being direct)
Are you afraid that your dad still will not accept you for who you are?

BEN
(Worried)
Well, yeah, I guess so. The last time my dad spoke to me, he was very angry.

CHARLES
(Being helpful)
One thing I have learned while being in treatment is that we have limited control over people, places, and situations.

BEN
(Uneasy)
I know, but it would mean the world to me if my dad would just hug me and tell me he loves me.

MARTY
(Being hopeful)
Who knows, maybe your father has had a change of heart.

BEN
(Hopeful)
Thanks, guys, I appreciate that you're trying to cheer me up.

CHARLES
(Encouraging)
Hang in there, Ben. It'll be okay.

MARTY
(Encouraging)
Remember don't quit before the miracle happens.

(Charles and Marty leave. Ben continues sitting on the bench, thinking. Ben sings [Song Selection].)

Read My Lips, Spiritual Awakening

(Scene 6: Dining Area)

STEVE
(Sincerity)

Look, Pazmate, you seem to have an issue with me. I don't know where it stems from—however, I'm hoping we can resolve it.

PAZMATE
(Sarcastically)

Steve, what would make you think I would waste my valuable time having an issue with you?

STEVE

Remarks like that.

PAZMATE
(Still in attack mode)

Well, excuse me! I will attempt to bring myself down to *your* level of class.

STEVE
(Irritated but calm)

I may not have as much money as you or come from a financially wealthy family, but when it comes to class, you know what—forget it. I'm not even going to go there with you. I'm just trying to call a truce here.

PAZMATE
(Not letting it go)

Truce? Aren't you the one who walks around here like a junior counselor? Seeming to have the answers for what is wrong with the rest of us?

STEVE
(Trying to explain himself)

You're right. I've been avoiding my personal issues by deflecting others. But now I'm trying to be honest with myself and my peers.

PAZMATE
(Smirking)

Good. You're a *real* good junior counselor. You know for a moment there I was actually falling for your clever, out-of-body spiritual awakening. Real good, counselor.

STEVE
(More assertive)

Read my lips: I'm not trying to con you. You flatter yourself if you think screwing with you means more to me than my own personal recovery. But I do feel that if we would start getting honest with each other, our treatment group would be a stronger unit.

PAZMATE
(Change of attitude)

Well, maybe you're right, Steve. Believe it or not, I'm really learning something here.

STEVE
(Direct)

So do we have a truce?

(Extending his hand)

PAZMATE

Truce.

(Pazmate accepts Steve's hand.)

PAZMATE

Hey, would you like to know something?

STEVE

Sure.

PAZMATE
(With humor)

Being filthy rich, handsome, and extremely smart isn't all it's cracked up to be.

STEVE
(Dramatic nod rubbing his chin and pointing to his temple)

I guess I'll have to take your word for it. I've learned to settle for two out of three.

PAZMATE
(Trying to be apologetic)

Ya know, no one has to tell me—I know at times I've been a jerk, but between you and me—I think you're alright, Steve.

STEVE
(Empathetically)

You're not so bad yourself (jokingly), once you pull your head out of the clouds.

PAZMATE
(Happy)

Hey, you know you can take honesty too far. Anyway, I need to go work on my relapse prevention project. Catch you later.

(Exits)

STEVE

Yeah, catch you later.

(Exits in opposite direction)

(As Pazmate walks toward his room, he sings [Song Selection].)

ACT III:
I CAN SEE CLEARLY NOW THE RAIN IS GONE

(Scene 1: Counselor's Office)

SKEETY
(Says upon entering)
Mike, I hope you're ready to start your lecture on time because I noticed all the clients were walking toward the group room, and we know how our clients enjoy watching the staff in hopes that they catch one of us slipping up by showing up late for group.

(Enter Inky)

MIKE
I'm feeling you on that, Skeety. After all these years of working in this field, I still find the amount of time clients spend observing the staff's every move, instead of investing that time into their personal recovery, interesting.

INKY
Excuse me, folks, but both of you are talking as if our clients come into treatment with healthy life skills and boundaries.

SKEETY
(Thinking about Inky's statement)
Yeah, I suppose you are right, but don't these clients get on your nerves even a little, Inky?

INKY
Most definitely!

MIKE
(Friendly debating)

Well, thanks for the class on proper ethics, Inky! However, the last time I checked, expressing feelings with your colleagues in a comfortable confident way, is considered to be healthy and ethical.

INKY
(Jokingly)

Absolutely! That is why I'm confident in keeping my adorable colleagues grounded to the fact of why they are here.

SKEETY
(Smiling)

Mike, how did we even allow ourselves to be suckered into this conversation with him?

MIKE
(Jokingly sarcastic)

Don't get me started, Skeety. I guess that's what happens when you're not busy working during the day, such as you and I. Judging from Inky's example, if you're not doing anything, you'll have time to think of a lot of things to poke your colleagues with.

SKEETY

I can see that!

(Singing)

I can see clearly now the rain is gone.

INKY
(Feeling the tune)

Wow, Skeety who sings that song? I haven't heard that groove in awhile.

SKEETY

I'm sorry, Inky. I can't seem to think of the artist right off the top of my head, but it's a pretty song, huh?

INKY
(Jokingly)

It *was* until *you* started singing it. Well, at least we all now know who doesn't sing it.

SKEETY
(Laughing)

Yeah, you have jokes.

INKY
(Bragging)

I thought you knew! Lendell L. *Jones* doesn't even have jokes like this.

MIKE
(In stitches)

Y'all are having too much fun in here. Let me get up out of here and go do my lecture on self-esteem. You guys are gonna make me pass out.

(Mike Exits)

Client Discussion

(Scene 2: Group Room)

(Clients are having a conversation before the counselor arrives.)

CHARLES
(Addressing the group without a counselor present)
Here we go again. Another stupid lecture.

SHARON
Do these counselors really think they're helping us?

PAZMATE
I doubt it. They're only here to collect a paycheck. I am willing to bet a popsicle that most of the counselors here drink and get high.

BEN
(Blurting)
Has it occurred to any of you that maybe the counselors here are trying to help us?

MINNIE
(In a good mood)
Maybe. You could be right, Ben, but to be honest with you, there isn't anything these counselors can teach me that I cannot learn on my block.

STEVE
(With compassion)
Perhaps the teachings you received from your block are the wrong kind of education.

MINNIE
Yeah, I feel you.

TERRY

I never thought I would ever be this happy to be in treatment.

MARTY
(Shyly)

My attitude is: as long as I'm here, the wise thing for me to do is try to gain something out of it.

PETE
(Annoyed)

You guys can be quiet now. Here comes the counselor.

JULIANNE
(Confronting Charles)

Personally, I enjoy gaining the new information I receive from the lectures. I don't think they are stupid at all.

Building Self-esteem

(Scene 3: Group Room)

MIKE
(Addressing clients)
Good evening, folks. How is everyone doing today?

STEVE
I'm doing well, how are you?

MIKE
(Observant)
I'm doing well also, Steve. Thanks for asking. Now that we have our formal greetings out of the way, let's get down to business. Today's topics will primarily focus on self-esteem.

MARTY
(To Mike)
What's self-esteem?

MIKE
Good question, Marty. Would anyone of you like to share with the group what self-esteem is?

PAZMATE
(Blurts)
Self-esteem is the way a person feels about themselves.

SHARON
(Interested)
What does self-esteem have to do with recovery?

BEN

Think about it, Sharon. If a person has good self-esteem, they would not entertain the desire to use in order to change their mood.

CHARLES

I'm the first to admit to have used substance, but I have good self-esteem. I feel very good about myself.

(Charles becomes a little defensive.)

JULIANNE
(Confrontational)

Charles, if you feel so good about yourself, why would you risk going to jail and prison along with neglecting your own family and putting yourself in dangerous situations in order to use?

PETE

Well, I'm not sure about the rest of you, but as for me, I have a lot of self-confidence! I recently was promoted by my company and I for one, can build almost anything with my hands.

(Pete shows the group his working man's hands.)

TERRY
(Correcting Pete)

I hope you realize that there's a difference between self-confidence and self-esteem.

CHARLES
(Sarcastic)

Oh, really? Please don't stop, Terry. Enlighten us.

TERRY
(Assertive)

Self-confidence, is your competence to do something, or your skills. Self-esteem is how you feel about yourself.

MIKE

Good. Good feedback from all of you. So, for those of you who would like to take notes during the lecture please feel free to do so.

(After completing the lecture Mike asks the group for any questions.)

Any questions?

(With no questions the group ends with, "Hope for a Better Day.")

We're Precious Souls

(Scene 4: Clients' Lounge)

SHARON
Hey, Ben. You have a moment?

BEN
Sure. What's on your mind?

SHARON
(Sincere)
Mike asked me to apologize to you for calling you a derogatory name.

BEN
(Calm)
You mean for calling me a faggot? Don't even worry over it. I've been called worse.

SHARON
(Doesn't understand Ben's calmness)
Yeah, I'll bet. But still, it wasn't right for me to be rude to you like that.

BEN
(Forgiving smile)
Sharon, please don't beat yourself up over what you called me. Sometimes we all say and do things that we later regret doing.

SHARON
(Being honest)
Ya know, some of the people I know would have a major problem with you and I havin' a civil conversation together.

BEN
(With a blank expression)
So tell me: how do *you* feel about us having a civil conversation?

SHARON
(Confused)
Honestly, I don't know how I feel. However, I'm sure that I would like to stop having so much anger toward other people.

BEN
(Concerned)
So how are you working on that?

SHARON
(A little emotional)
My counselor has allowed me to explore myself by giving me exercise materials to work on and he encourages me to identify with my core feelings.

BEN
(Happy)
Good for you, Sharon. As for me, the therapeutic groups and lectures have really helped. For the first time in my life, I feel okay in my own skin. I think that's why what you said doesn't really bother me anymore.

SHARON
(Sincere)
That's nice, Ben. We've spent too much time lying to ourselves. We're not misfits, ya know? I think we're all precious souls.

BEN
(Smiling)

You've got that right, friend girl.

SHARON

I'm really glad you accepted my apology. I think you are a beautiful person, but I have to get goin' now and head towards my women's group before I'm late again. Thanks again for forgiving me. I'll catch you later.

(Sharon exits, singing [Song Selection].)

BEN

I completely forgive you. I'll talk to you later. Bye.

(Ben exits in opposite direction.)

It's Time to Get Honest

(Scene 5: Outside Bench Area)

STEVE
(Expressing happiness for Charles)
Hey, Charles. You did good work in the therapeutic group today. You shared a lot. It took some guts to get that honest. How do you feel?

CHARLES
(Feeling good)
You know, I still can't believe I opened up that much. But as I began sharing my story and the group allowed me to feel comfortable, I knew it was time for me to be honest with myself and others.

PAZMATE
I remember the first time I opened up with the group. I had a lot of mixed feelings. I didn't know if I was coming or going. But once I got all that garbage out, I felt so much better.

MARTY
You still haven't answered Steve's question—how do you feel Charles?

CHARLES
(Genuine)
I feel good. Man do I feel good! I'm still a little shaky from the group experience, I gotta admit.

MARTY
(With compassion)
I'm glad you decided to get real with the group. We're not here to judge. We are all here just trying to get better for ourselves and our families.

STEVE
(Direct)
That's right. We all know the way our lives were before treatment.

PETE
(Encouraging)
I didn't realize how angry I was until I started to get honest with myself and others. Now, by taking a risk and sharing how I really feel during the therapeutic groups along with opening up to my primary counselor, I can honestly say that I look toward the future with "hope for a better day."

PAZMATE
This recovery stuff can't be all that bad, I mean, I never heard of anyone going to jail or losing their families and jobs because they were too clean and sober.

CHARLES
(Understanding)
I suppose you are right. I just always thought being clean and sober was for squares that lived a boring life.

PETE
(Being honest)
I understand. I used to think if I came to treatment, the counselors would try to brainwash me!

MARTY
(With confidence)
It's funny that you said that Pete, because that's what I told Charles a few weeks ago, "If it takes brainwashing for me to live a happy joyous life, I hope the counselors brainwash the hell out of me!"

STEVE

Whoop, there it is!

PAZMATE
(Empathetic)

Whoop, there it is!

PETE
(Joining in)

Whoop, there it is!

CHARLES
(In a good mood)

Perhaps me coming to treatment and learning more about the dangers and consequences of substance abuse turns out to be a good thing for me.

PAZMATE

Why do you say "perhaps"?

STEVE
(Pushing Charles)

Should we review what life was like before treatment?

CHARLES
(Letting go)

Okay, okay! I admit—coming to treatment has been beneficial for me. Are you happy now?

MARTY

I've been happy for a while now. How about you? Are you happy?

CHARLES

Yeah, I am.

PETE

Good. On that note, it's getting late and I need to finish up my communication skills project.

(Says goodbye and exits)

CHARLES

Well, I hate to bail on you cats too, but I have kitchen detail and I need to get busy. I'll catch up with you guys later. See ya!

(Charles high-fives the rest of the guys and exits.)

What is the Good Stuff?

(Scene 6: Group Room)

SKEETY
Okay, ladies. Today our topic will focus on: "What is the good stuff?"

MINNIE
(With passion)
For me, the good stuff is having someone love me just for who I am and don't keep throwing my past up in my face!

JULIANNE
(With sadness)
My idea of the good stuff is having my children back in my custody and not losing them again because of my lifestyle.

TERRY
(Hopeful)
The good stuff to me means accepting my past and facing the future with hope and enthusiasm.

SHARON
(Finally invested in her treatment)
It's takin' responsibility for my own actions and feelings. That's the good stuff.

SKEETY
Good job, ladies. For your next question: If you had only twenty-four hours to live, who would you like to be with? And what would you do?

(Allows time for reflection)

JULIANNE
(Eyes watering)

I would be with my children and I think I'd just hold them. I'd talk with them and reassure them how much I love them.

TERRY

I would spend my last twenty-four hours with the homeless, encouraging them that there is hope for a better day.

MINNIE
(Nostalgic)

All my time would be shared with my brother and sister, reminiscing over the values and teachings we all received from our parents.

SHARON
(With a big smile)

I would spend the last twenty-four hours of my life with family members. Tell them about all the wonderful things I've learned while in treatment.

SKEETY
(Taking a moment for reflection)

Alright, ladies. Here's your last question for this exercise: Who or what would you not want to do in your last twenty-four hours?

TERRY

Not loaded. I wouldn't want that.

JULIANNE

Being without my children is the saddest thing I can think of.

SHARON
(A little sad)

Going back to my old thoughts and behaviors. I'm so sick of it. I would not want to spend my last twenty-four hours on earth that way.

MINNIE
(Inspired)

I would not want to live my last twenty-four hours doing nothing. I'd stay busy enjoying my life to the very end.

SKEETY

Okay. Good job, ladies. You all did good work today. I witnessed some of you becoming emotional when sharing sensitive feelings and that's okay. Recovery is about recovering those feelings that have been hidden away for so long. Remember, one of the first things that come back once you begin to recover is buried feelings. Does anyone have something they would like to add before we close group?

(The group shakes their heads.)

SKEETY

Okay. Then let's close with, "Hope for a Better Day."

ACT IV: HE DOESN'T SEEM RIGHT

(Scene 1: Counselors' Treatment Office)

SKEETY
(Pleasantly)

Hi, Mike!

MIKE
(Quickly)

Hey.

INKY

Some of the staff will be going to Snappy's Barbeque for lunch. Would you like to join us?

MIKE
(Indifferent)

No thanks, Inky. I have too much work to do around here.

INKY
(Concerned)

Mike, are you okay? You seem to be, I don't know, isolating.

MIKE
(Laughing it off)

Come on, guys. I'm just busy. Maybe I'm due for a vacation.

SKEETY
(Joking behind concern)

You? Take time away from work? That would be the day!

INKY

I don't know how you do it. You must be a machine or something.

MIKE
(Small sense of humor)

No, I'm just a man—with 'super' in front.

SKEETY
(Being direct)

Are you sure you're doing okay? Have you lost weight?

MIKE
(Smiling but irritated)

I'm fine. I'm fine!

INKY
(Concerned by Mike's shortness)

Okay. If you say so. Oh, before I forget, Sharon was looking for you earlier.

MIKE
(Seems a little excited)

Sharon, huh? She has really made progress toward her recovery.

SKEETY
(Suspicious)

Would you like for us to order you something to eat while we're at Snappy's?

MIKE
(Rubbing his stomach)

I think I'll decline, Skeety. I had a big breakfast this morning before coming to work.

INKY

Huh, I wonder where it all went.

MIKE
(Frustrated)

With that, that's my cue to go to my office and get to work. You all have a great lunch.

(Mike exits)

SKEETY
(Concerned)

I think something is wrong with Mike.

INKY
(In agreement)

He doesn't seem right, does he?

(Skeety and Inky sing [Song Selection].)

Hope for a Better Day

(Scene 2: Mike's Office)

MIKE
(With a pleasant tone)
Sharon, come on in. How are you doing? Grab a seat. I was told you were looking for me earlier. How can I assist you?

SHARON
(Respectfully)
I just wanted to let you know I completed all of my assignments and tomorrow when I discharge from treatment, I feel I'm ready to live life on life's terms.

MIKE
(Pleased)
Great! I think you'll do well back in your community.

SHARON
(Reluctant and grateful)
Mike—I know my attitude wasn't very good when I first arrived here, but I sincerely would like to thank you for allowing me to grow at my own pace.

MIKE
(Touched)
I'm proud of you. It took much courage to explore new ideas and the willingness to change old behaviors.

SHARON
(Sincere)
As you know, I didn't exactly want to be here, but when I began to take responsibility and look at myself, I was able to get honest about what was going on inside of me.

MIKE
(Direct)

So share with me. When you arrive back into your community, what are some of the goals you've set in order to support your recovery?

SHARON

Well, I know I'm gonna get into twelve-step meetings 'cause I prove to myself that I can't stay clean and sober alone. Most importantly, I need to work on a program and not just show up for meetings.

MIKE

How difficult do you think it's going to be when your old associates realize you have a new attitude toward people, places, and things?

SHARON

Are you referring to my White Knight family?

MIKE

Yes, I am Sharon.

SHARON
(Honest)

To tell ya the truth, I don't know how I'm going to handle that situation.

MIKE

Do you feel that your life may be in danger?

SHARON
(Concerned but brave)

Right now all I need to think about is living one day at a time.

MIKE
(Pleased)

It seems that you've invested in treatment quite well.

SHARON
(Happy)
Thanks to this program I feel I have a chance to live a joyous happy life.

MIKE
(Smiling)
Remember, you create your own happiness.

SHARON
Thank you so much, Mike, for all your support.

(Sharon stands up, shakes Mike's hand, and exits his office.)

MIKE
Good luck, Sharon.

(Watches her leave)

Family Reunion

(Scene 3: Outside Bench Area)

TERRY
(Poking fun)
So, how was it? Don't keep us in suspense.

BEN
(Excited)
He said he loves me!

TERRY
Oh, that's wonderful news, Ben.

(Holds Ben's hands)
See, you were all worried for nothing.

BEN
(More excited)
My mom, she loves me too!

MINNIE
(Smiling)
So how's your pops feeling?

BEN
(Saddened)
He said he's doing well, but—he didn't look so well.

TERRY
(Concerned)
I'm sorry, Ben.

BEN
I guess this happy reunion was also a sad one.

MINNIE
(Expressing her condolences)

I'm sorry. I didn't mean to bring you down.

TERRY
(With compassion)

What about your mom? How is she holding up?

BEN
(Spirits lifted)

Mom—she always has been a strong person. She won't let Dad see how scared and sad she is. Mom has always been the stone in our family.

MINNIE
(Attentive)

So what did you and your pops talk about? Is he still ashamed of you?

BEN
(Brightening up)

He still doesn't agree with my lifestyle, but he said he forgave me about three years ago. He just didn't know how to tell me.

TERRY

That's great!

BEN
(Chuckling)

Guess what, Minnie!

MINNIE
(Puzzled)

What?

BEN
(Big smile)

My parents want me to move in with them after I complete treatment. That way I can help Mom around the house and assist her with taking care of Dad.

TERRY

See, your family does love you.
(Terry gives Ben a big hug).

BEN
(Emotional)

Thanks. You guys are also like family to me.

MINNIE
(Picking on Ben)

Oh, no. Watch out, Terry. Ben's ready to start that mushy stuff.

BEN

I really mean it!
(Ben playfully slaps at Minnie.)

TERRY
(Comforting Ben)

We know you're sincere. I want you to know you have been a support for us too.

MINNIE
(Happy for Ben)

I'm just glad that you and your pop made up.

TERRY
(Smiling)

Me too.

BEN
(Emotional)
When I leave here I'm really going to miss you guys.

MINNIE
Well, if you ever feel brave, you know where to find me, 112 W. Elm Street. Holla!

(Minnie gives Ben a big hug.)

TERRY
I gave you my phone number. Give me a call sometime. I'll really appreciate that.

(Terry grabs both Ben's hands again)

We love you.

BEN
(Sincere)
I love you guys, too.

It's Called Bipolar

(Scene 4: Outside Clients' Work Bench)

PAZMATE
(Looking around)

Hey, has anyone seen Julianne?

PETE
(Points him in the right direction)

I've just seen her working on her parenting assignment at the outside work table.

PAZMATE
(Nods)

Thanks, Pete.

PAZMATE
(Says upon approach)

Julianne, have you forgotten? You're on dishwashing detail this week.

JULIANNE
(Sarcastic)

Who do you think you are, my father?

PAZMATE
(Snaps back)

No, I am not your father, but I am the clients' president this week and one of my responsibilities is to remind people to do their chores.

JULIANNE
(Rudely)

Whoa! Sorry Mr. Rich Guy. I bet you really enjoy the power.

PAZMATE
(Disturbed by her attitude)

What's wrong with you? This morning during breakfast you were the most pleasant person at the meal table. Now you seem like you want to rip my head off.

JULIANNE
(Snotty)

It's called bipolar disorder and if you must know, my emotions are out of whack. Half the time I don't know if I'm coming or going.

PAZMATE
(Sincere)

Aren't you taking medication for that?

JULIANNE
(Anxious)

Yes, and I hate it. The medication seems to make me feel worse.

PAZMATE

Have you talked with your primary counselor about your feelings?
(Pazmate sits down beside Julianne.)

JULIANNE
(Upset with her counselor)

Yeah, I have and all she says is to give the medicine time to work.

PAZMATE
(Comforting)

Julianne, if talking to your primary counselor isn't working for you, your other option is going to the facility doctor and talking to him about your medication concerns.

JULIANNE
(Weakly smiling)
I know.

PAZMATE
So are you?

JULIANNE
(Being pleasant)
No. I think I'll take my primary counselor's advice and take the medication a few more days.

PAZMATE
(Still a little hurt by Julianne's prior attitude)
Well, I hope the medicine starts working fast for you, Julianne, because I don't know what to expect from you hour to hour.

JULIANNE
(Sincere)
I'm sorry, Pazmate.

PAZMATE
(Smiles)
All's forgiven.

JULIANNE
(Being playful)
I always knew underneath that uppity, snooty, and arrogant shield, there was a real person.

PAZMATE
(Jokingly)
Hey, Julianne. Don't think flattery is going to get you out of dish detail.

JULIANNE
(Batting her eyes)
Pazzzz, can't you do it for me?

PAZMATE
(Batting his eyes)
I don't think so. Bye, Julianne.

JULIANNE
Man, you're tough.

The Future is Looking Bright

(Scene 5: Male Clients' Room)

(The male clients share a conversation in their bedroom right before they go to sleep.)

PETE
(Lying on his bed)

I can't believe it. In a few days, I will have completed this program.

MARTY
(Sitting on his bed)

I know. Time has flown.

CHARLES
(Standing by his bed)

Yeah, it's funny. I really didn't expect to learn anything. To my own surprise, I have learned a lot about the road to recovery.

PETE
(Happy)

Me too.

CHARLES
(Looking at Steve)

What about you, counselor? I bet you knew all this stuff already.

STEVE
(Exercising on the floor)

You're right, Charles. I knew a lot about the tools to recovery. Now by coming to treatment, I'm finally learning how to apply them.

MARTY
(Boldly)

I still find it hard to believe how confident I've been feeling about myself lately.

PETE
(Joyous)

It's kind of strange how confident I feel about myself and managing my anger issues. It's almost as if I had a spiritual awakening.

CHARLES

Before coming here and gaining insight about myself, I was convinced the way I was living was the only way.

STEVE
(Hopeful)

It's amazing how clear things became for me—once I removed the blinders from my eyes and took the cotton out of my ears.

MARTY
(Excited)

The first thing I'm going to do when I get back home is call my sponsor and ask him to teach me how to work the twelve steps to recovery.

PETE

I hear ya, Marty. The first thing I'm going to do when I get back is go to a twelve-step meeting.

CHARLES
(Confident)

Me, I'm calling my ex-employer and see if I can get my old job back.

MARTY
(Surprised)

Back in the oil field?

CHARLES
(With a big smile)

Yep.

MARTY
(Expressing concern)

Isn't that kind of risky, being that you're just getting out of treatment? You know the oil field has a reputation for substance abuse.

CHARLES

Look here, my little friend, substance abuse is everywhere, but I'm here to tell you those safety guys are everywhere in the oil field. So it's not as bad as many people think it is out there.

PETE
(Understanding)

Charles is right, Marty. Our personal recovery has to come first. However, we also have to earn a living.

STEVE

I think I'll go back to school and work on a new career.

MARTY
(Curious)

Whatcha have in mind?

STEVE
(Like a free spirit)

I don't know where my new road will lead me. I'll figure it out as long as I take life's new adventures one day at a time.

(Charles, Marty, Pete, and Steve all sing [Song Selection].)

PAZMATE
(Sits up in bed, sleepily)

Hey, I'm really touched over you guys' little family reunion, but you all need to turn the volume off and go to sleep.

BEN
(Also sleepy)

I second that motion.

STEVE
(Happy)

Good night.

MARTY
(Joyous)

Good night.

PETE
(Peaceful)

Good night.

CHARLES
(Hopeful)

Good night.

Is this the End?

(Scene 6: Treatment Office)

SKEETY
(Full of joy)

Good morning.

INKY
(Taking a second look at Skeety)

Good morning, you look sharp as a tack.

SKEETY
(Spins and smiles)

Thanks. I don't know what got into me. I just felt this need to dress up this morning.

INKY

So, what aftercare program are you setting your two graduating clients up with?

(Inky walks toward the discharge board to write down Skeety's information.)

SKEETY

Mission Impossible Counseling. They deserve the best!

INKY

True enough. It doesn't get any better than M.I.C.
(Administrator Tim enters)

SKEETY
(Greeting administrator)

This is a nice surprise. We usually don't have the pleasure of seeing the administrator out of his office until noon.

INKY
(Kissing up)

Don't worry about her. It's always good to see you, Tim.

TIM

Please close the door.
(Inky shuts the treatment office door. Tim has a strange look about him.)

INKY
(Concerned)

Tim, you're smiling really big. What's up?

TIM
(Joyful)

I have some good news.

SKEETY
(Questionably excited)

What?

INKY
(Anxious)

What is it, Tim?

TIM
(Fast and happy)

Mike has been selected Behavioral Health Counselor of the Year. Voted by the National Health Board.

SKEETY
(Happy disbelief)

You've got to be kidding me.

TIM
(Smiling)

Seriously. I'm not kidding at all.

SKEETY
(Laughing)
Oh my goodness! That's so great.

INKY
(In delighted shock)
How, how could Mike earn such a prestigious honor?

TIM
(Trying to be calm)
My understanding is, the Behavioral Health Board has been tracking clients' progress after they leave residential treatment. After completing their research, they discovered 80 percent of Mike's clients have remained clean and sober over the past eighteen months.

SKEETY
(Pleased)
I can't believe this. I would have never thought Mike was that committed to helping his clients.

TIM
(Sharing Skeety's amazement)
No one in our agency knew Mike was doing such a great job.

INKY
Tim, when did you find out he was selected?

TIM
Only hours before coming to work this morning. I received a phone call from the President of the Behavioral Health Board herself.

SKEETY
This is so strange. Mike just doesn't seem to be himself lately. Inky and I thought something was wrong with him.

INKY

I guess we as professionals should take notes on Mike's success. He has shown us that by working patiently with your clients, good things are bound to happen.

(Inky is shaking his head and is visibly happy.)

TIM

If anyone is interested, I have arranged to take Mike to the Bluffs Saturday evening at 7:00 for a congratulatory supper. You're both welcome to join us.

SKEETY

Today is the day that treatment cries the blues with *joyful* tears.

(The administrator and counselors sing [Song Selection] as they celebrate Mike's success.)

Alternative Ending

(**Scene 6:** Treatment Office)

SKEETY
(Full of joy)

Good morning.

INKY
(Taking a second look at Skeety)

Good morning, you look sharp as a tack.

SKEETY
(Spins and smiles)

Thanks. I don't know what got into me. I just felt this need to dress up this morning.

INKY

So, what aftercare program are you setting your two graduating clients up with?

(Inky walks toward the discharge board to write down Skeety's information.)

SKEETY

Mission Impossible Counseling. They deserve the best!

INKY

I know that's right. It doesn't get any better than M.I.C.
(Administrator Tim enters)

SKEETY
(Greeting administrator)

This is a nice surprise. We usually don't have the pleasure of seeing the administrator out of his office until noon.

INKY
(Kissing up)
Don't worry about her. It's always good to see you, Tim.

TIM
Please close the door.
(Inky shuts the treatment office door. Tim has a strange look about him.)

INKY
(Concerned)
Tim, you don't look well. What's wrong?

TIM
(Sadness)
I have some bad news.

SKEETY
(Questionably excited)
What?

INKY
(Anxious)
What is it, Tim?

TIM
(Slow and sad)
Mike took his own life last night.

SKEETY
(Disbelief)
You've got to be kidding me. Please don't play like that.

TIM
(Fighting back tears)
Goodness knows. I wish I was playing. I'm not kidding at all.

SKEETY
(Crying)
Oh my goodness! I can't believe it.

INKY
(In tormented shock)
How, how did Mike do it?

TIM
(Trying to be calm)
My understanding is, he wrote a note to his family trying to explain then took a bottle of sleeping pills and never woke up again.

SKEETY
(Blank stare)
No! No! I would have never thought Mike could do such a thing. Why? Why did he do it?

TIM
(Sharing Skeety's pain)
No one knows why, Skeety. Mike has always worked well with his clients and other people.

INKY
(Struggling to ask)
Who found Mike like that?

TIM
(Slow and sad)
Only hours before coming to work. I received a phone call from his sister LaGail. She went to his home for coffee this morning and found him at the kitchen table.

SKEETY
(In a state of disbelief)

This is so strange. Mike just didn't seem to be himself lately. Inky and I thought something was wrong with him. He appeared distant and troubled the last several months.

TIM
(Crying)

I had uneasy feelings about Mike's behaviors lately too. I'm now embarrassed to say I didn't know what to do.

SKEETY
(Crying and yelling)

We are counselors! Why didn't any of us do something to prevent this?

INKY
(Visibly shaken)

I guess we as professionals, family members, and friends should take notes on Mike's tragedy. We all need to get ourselves educated about the warning signs when someone we know may be suicidal and learn how to intervene. What we know about suicide and prevention may save a life someday.

TIM
(Calm and steady)

If anyone is interested, I have arranged for a grief therapist to support anyone wanting help, while working through this unfortunate tragedy.

SKEETY
(Dazed and confused)

Thanks, you know when I came to work this morning I felt extremely joyful. Now I feel like today is the day that treatment cries the blues.

(The administrator and counselors sing [Song Selection] as a remembrance to Mike.)

ABOUT THE AUTHOR

Lendell L. Jones resides in Farmington, New Mexico where he works in the field of substance abuse and behavioral health. He dealt with substance abuse in his youth and became homeless as he diminished to living in shelters, abandoned buildings, and trains before resolving. At the age of twenty-five, he began his journey toward personal recovery and began a mission to help other people and families troubled by addiction. Since earning his substance abuse license in 1998, Lendell has founded Mission Impossible Counseling, an outpatient substance-abuse agency. Lendell accredits much of his works to real-life experiences.

Lendell first put his writing skills to the test in 2000 when he wrote his first professional presentation entitled, "The Core Value of Self-Esteem," which is among the favorites presented in treatment and counseling centers throughout the nation. He then followed up with the powerful presentation, "Level 1, 2, and 3" in 2001. He went on to release his third presentation, "It's a Thin Line Between Healthy and Unhealthy Relationships" in 2002. Lendell took his writing skills in a different direction in 2003 as he created the stage play, "Treatment Cries the Blues." After enjoying its success, he followed up in 2004 by writing the stage play "Smoke-free in Maroon Village." Lendell's excitement for therapeutic growth is not limited to writing. He developed the phenomenal therapeutic board game, "High Life" in 2005. In 2006, Lendell created the Level II education and therapy DUI curriculums, Vapor I, and in 2007 he wrote PACE (Parents and

Children Evolving) curriculum. In 2013, Lendell released, "Partners: an Intimate (therapeutic) Couples Game." This game is designed to help couples strengthen their relationships.

In 2020 Lendell developed VAPOR Anger. VAPOR Anger is an organized motivational program that Specifically addresses "out of control anger". VAPOR Anger accepts the truth rather than collusion. The program is designed to allow participants who are seeking help for "out of control anger" to freely express daily positive and negative stressors as they discover they are not alone in their "out of control anger" struggles.

www.ingramcontent.com/pod-product-compliance
Lightning Source LLC
LaVergne TN
LVHW041802060526
838201LV00046B/1094